What people are sayin

I'm excited to recommend *Believer's* .... goes to the heart of the matter and lays the foundation for a life of victory, freedom, and total success, with practical, straightforward steps to activate your God-given authority. It's amazing to me that as much as authority is taught in the Bible, very few people ever really experience it, let alone exercise it in their own lives. Why does authority matter? Because once you know who you are and what you can do, Satan has no power over you. As you read this book, you'll be energized and stirred up to enforce the authority you've had all along to tell Satan that he no longer has a right to interfere with anything you do. This book is a life-changer, a must-read for every believer!

—*Dr. Jesse Duplantis*
Host, *Jesse Duplantis* TV show

I'm glad to recommend *Believer's Authority*. Brother Happy and his wife, Jeanne, have been used of the Lord for decades to lead many people to victory over every kind of problem. Believers who don't know of their authority in Christ, and how to exercise it, are easily overcome and held in bondage to the enemy's many devices. But when the child of God realizes the amazing authorization and empowerment that Jesus, at such great cost, has provided, their oppressed days are over! And when we obtain our own freedom, we can begin to be used by God to set others free, as well. As you read this book, ask the Lord to open your eyes and bring you into an operating knowledge of these wonderful truths.

—*Keith Moore*
President, Moore Life Ministries

Happy Caldwell is one of the finest teachers in the body of Christ. In his new book, *Believer's Authority*, he outlines principle after principle, line upon line, the truths God's Word teaches us concerning our authority as believers, and the absolute necessity for every believer to exercise that authority. Too many Christians today are allowing the devil to run rampant through their lives. There is a way to live your life in victory, and to beat the devil at every turn. Happy's book will fully equip you to overcome the devil and keep him in the one place he belongs—under your feet. It's the truth you know that sets you free, and Jesus paid the ultimate price for your freedom. Don't give the devil one more inch of space in your life. Put on the authority Jesus purchased for you. Walk it out, and watch what God will accomplish in you and for you every single day!

—*Dr. Jerry Savelle*
President, Jerry Savelle Ministries International

Dr. Happy Caldwell's life and ministry have been based on the foundation of the *Believer's Authority* given to us in the Word of God. His ministry reaches across America and around the world as a living portrait of the power of authority to accomplish the purposes of God. You will enjoy every page of *Believer's Authority*!

—*Pastor John Hagee*
Cornerstone Church

I have known Happy Caldwell since 1977. Without any hesitation, I can say that Happy is a man who loves God and lives by His Word. I am so thankful that he has written *Believer's Authority*, because understanding and walking in godly authority is vital to living a life of faith in Jesus Christ, and for fulfilling the call of God upon one's life. This book has blessed me; I know it will bless you, too.

—*Pat Harrison*
President and founder,
Faith Christian Fellowship International Church, Inc.

Without a doubt, I believe the worst doctrine in the body of Christ today is the fatalistic thinking that God controls everything that happens to us. This leads to passivity and submission to things that are completely outside of God's will for us. Millions of people have turned against a God they think has caused or allowed all the hurt in their lives. The antidote to this wrong thinking is a revelation of the authority God has given every believer. Happy has hit the nail on the head. I've seen the results of what Happy teaches in his life and ministry. It works. It will work for you, too.

—*Andrew Wommack*
Andrew Wommack Ministries

Believer's AUTHORITY

HAPPY Caldwell

WHITAKER
HOUSE

BELIEVER'S AUTHORITY:
Taking Dominion over Sin, Sickness, Poverty, and Death

Pastor Happy Caldwell
Agape Church, Inc.
P.O. Box 22007,
Little Rock, AR 72221–2007
www.agape-church.org

ISBN: 978-1-60374-277-1
eBook ISBN: 978-1-60374-896-4
Printed in the United States of America
© 2013 by Happy Caldwell

Whitaker House
1030 Hunt Valley Circle
New Kensington, PA 15068
www.whitakerhouse.com

Library of Congress Cataloging-in-Publication Data (Pending)

1 2 3 4 5 6 7 8 9 10 ⊞ 19 18 17 16 15 14 13

DEDICATION

This book is dedicated to heroes of the faith throughout history who paved the way for today's believers to discover their incredible authority in Christ. Your uncompromising stand on the truth of God's Word has caused a tidal wave of blessings throughout the world.

Thank you!

CONTENTS

All things are possible to him who believes.
—Mark 9:23

1

WHY AUTHORITY MATTERS

From the beginning of creation to the ministry of Jesus and throughout the church age, there is no message more revolutionary, life-changing, or misunderstood than a believer's authority on the earth. Yet many believers are totally ignorant of the amazing authority God has given them. Most believe they are just hapless pilgrims trudging through the hardships of life. With a philosophy of "God is in control" and "whatever will be, will be," they don't think there's anything they can do to improve their situation.

Perhaps you are among the countless Christians who have adopted this erroneous worldview. Instead of recognizing your rights as a believer, you've embraced predestination or fatalism, assuming you must simply accept your circumstances as God's will for your life. If that dismal mind-set isn't working very well for you, this book may be exactly what you need. God's truth will make you free (see John 8:32) and bring you into a wonderful new life of hope, healing, and provision.

If you search the Scriptures, you will discover that God's desire has *always* been to bless His people. He is a loving heavenly Father, and He has entrusted His divine authority to us as His sons and daughters. This is a central part of our mandate and our commission, and He will judge us accordingly.

From the garden of Eden, where God made man in His image (see Genesis 1:26–28), to the book of Revelation, where He calls us *"kings and priests"* (Revelation 1:6), we see the incredible authority God gave to us as believers. *"We shall reign on the earth"* (Revelation 5:10) is a repeated theme from Adam to Abraham and from Joshua to Jesus.

When Jesus told Peter that He was giving him *"the keys of the kingdom of heaven"* (Matthew 16:19), He was saying, in effect, "I'm giving you authority to operate on the earth like we operate in heaven." And even Job was taught by God to discard his faulty thinking and receive a miraculous breakthrough of healing and abundance.

Why the Ignorance?

Why are so many believers ignorant of their authority? Many reasons, I'm sure. First, Satan is intent on blinding people's minds. (See 2 Corinthians 4:4.) If he is unable to keep someone from being saved, he will at least try to keep them from being victorious and fruitful. The devil knows that believers who understand their authority in Christ will pose a major threat to his kingdom.

People have also been blinded and inoculated by religious tradition and erroneous teachings. They've been indoctrinated with the hopeless mind-set that everything they encounter in life is God's will for them. To them, resistance is futile!

And it's no wonder that this fatalistic outlook is appealing. You see, if everything that happens to us is God's will, then we are not responsible for the outcome. It's convenient to blame God rather than acknowledge that many things in life are the direct result of our faith or unbelief, our obedience or disobedience, or whether or not we've used our authority as believers.

You've probably heard a common statement that is widely believed but totally false: "What you don't know can't hurt you." Over decades of ministry, I've seen, over and over again, how tragically misguided this notion is. Every day, countless people are deeply hurt by what they simply didn't know.

This saddens the heart of Father God, for He wants His people to prosper, be in health, and live in victory in every area of their lives. In His Word, we're told that *"His divine power has given to us **all things** that pertain to life and godliness, through the knowledge of Him who called us by glory and virtue, by which have been given to us exceedingly great and precious promises"* (2 Peter 1:3–4).

What a powerful statement! God has given us *"exceedingly great and precious promises"* in His Word, and these promises are backed up by *"His divine power."* We don't have to live as paupers or victims, because He has given us *everything* we need for *"life and godliness."* Absolutely *nothing* is excluded from *"all things"*! God has given us the right to take authority over *anything* the Enemy sends our way.

This passage also says that God's amazing promises must be activated in our lives *"through the knowledge of Him."* The more you get to know your heavenly Father in an intimate way, the more you will be filled with faith and boldness to walk in His authority.

Incredible blessings are available to those who understand how to exercise the authority they have through their union with Christ. Poverty and sickness flee; Satan's strongholds of despair and hopelessness are cast down; and broken relationships are restored. All because we've finally grasped the authority of a believer!

Back to the Beginning

Giving authority to humankind is not some "new" idea. Rather, it was God's original intent for men and women to be His crowning glory and to exercise authority and dominion over His creation.

From the beginning of creation, God delegated His authority to humankind. He had the right to hold all authority, but He chose to give it to Adam and Eve, the first man and woman:

> *Then God said, "Let Us make man in Our image, according to Our likeness; let them have dominion over the fish of the sea, over the birds of the air, and over the cattle, over all the earth and over every creeping thing that creeps on the earth." So God created man in His own image; in the image of God He created him; male and female He created them. Then God blessed them, and God said to them, "Be fruitful and multiply; fill the earth and subdue it; have dominion over the fish of the sea, over the birds of the air, and over every living thing that moves on the earth."* (Genesis 1:26–28)

After creating us in His image and likeness, God gave us dominion over the earth and everything in it. He told us to *"be fruitful and multiply; fill the earth and subdue it."* The psalmist describes our original mandate this way: *"The heaven, even the heavens, are the* Lord's; *but the earth He has given to the children of men"* (Psalm 115:16). God made the earth and then gave it to us.

However, the authority given to humankind was *delegated* authority. The only reason Adam and Eve could exercise dominion over the earth was because they were *under* God's authority. As long as they submitted to Him, they could reign and rule over His creation.

"Dominion" is a very significant word. The dictionary defines it as "having the power to reign, rule, control, govern, subjugate, and dominate." It means having sovereign authority, similar to what a king exercises over his territory.

The clear message is this: God wants us to *"reign in life"* through our union with Christ (see Romans 5:17), and this means having dominion and victory in every area of our lives. Instead of being far off or out of reach, this is supposed to be the normal Christian life! God gives this amazing promise to each person who walks closely with Him and meditates on the precepts and promises of His Word: *"Whatever he does shall prosper"* (Psalm 1:1–3). Isn't that awesome?

Sabotaged by Unbelief

This life of victory is available to every child of God—but it's not automatic. Many people have been born again, with every right to live an abundant life. Yet their blessings have been forfeited and sabotaged by ignorance or unbelief. God says, *"My people are destroyed for lack of knowledge"* (Hosea 4:6).

What if your child is being tormented by a demon, but you insist that you don't believe in that "deliverance stuff"? Instead of taking authority over the demon, you end up medicating your child until he or she can hardly function.

What if you are constantly battling illness of one kind or another due to a spirit of infirmity? In Christ, you have authority over sickness, but will you rise to the occasion and *exercise* your authority as a believer? You don't have to let the devil stomp all over you!

When Satan tries to bring something into your family, take away your health, or steal your finances or your peace, you can take dominion over the situation. Instead of passively accepting the devil's attack, you can tell him, "No you don't, you outlaw spirit. You must get out of here. You have no right or authority in my home, my children, my bank account, or my health. In the name of Jesus, I have authority over you, and you must leave!"

And what if you're battling a spirit such as fear, lust, anger, or depression? Instead of tolerating the situation and resigning yourself, convincing yourself that you'll have to just "live with it," don't you want to have it cast out by someone who has faith in that area? You don't have to settle for less than God's best!

The bottom line is this: Those who don't understand their authority as believers are too often *"destroyed for lack of knowledge"* (Hosea 4:6). But this doesn't have to be the case with you, my friend. God has sent this book your way for a reason. If you grasp your incredible authority in Christ, a tidal wave of blessings will impact your life. And as a bonus, God will transform the lives of your friends and loved ones as you stand in faith on their behalf. (See Genesis 12:2.)

Your Day of New Beginnings

No matter what kind of life you've been living up to this point, today can be a new day—a turnaround day, a day of fabulous new beginnings.

Instead of being intimidated by the problems and obstacles you face, you can see them as wonderful opportunities to use mountain-moving faith. Jesus said that when you understand your authority, *"you will say to this mountain, 'Move from here to there,' and it will move; and nothing will be impossible for you"* (Matthew 17:20).

Take a minute to read Jesus' statement again, and really let it sink in this time. No matter how fierce a storm you are going through, Jesus says *"**nothing** will be impossible for you."* If you are truly a believer today, you can be confident that *"**all things** are possible to him who believes"* (Mark 9:23).

As you read this book, I pray that your faith will be stirred to rise up and seize the authority you've been given as God's beloved son or daughter. May you see that because God is *for you*, no problem can stand against you. (See Romans 8:31.) May you recognize that wherever your foot shall tread, He has *given you* that ground. (See Joshua 1:3.) And instead of fearing the enemy's attacks, may you go on the *offensive* by taking up *"the sword of the Spirit, which is the word of God"* (Ephesians 6:17).

It's time for a new generation of believers to arise. Throughout the earth, men and women of God must understand their authority in Christ and start using that authority in their daily lives. That's why I wrote this book.

So fasten your seat belt and get ready for an exciting, life-changing journey of faith!

2

THE PURPOSE OF OUR AUTHORITY

We see from Genesis 1:26–28 that God instituted authority as a critical ingredient in our calling as men and women. Just as He created us in His image and likeness, He also told us to subdue the earth and take dominion over it.

Understanding and operating in our authority as believers is not just an option from God—it's a mandate! There's no way to fully complete our commission from the Lord unless we are operating in His delegated authority. So I'm sure He's grieved when some Christians don't think His authority is something they really need.

I love the words of David in Psalm 24:1, but it's a passage some people have misinterpreted: *"The earth is the LORD's, and all its fullness, the world and those who dwell therein."* This has been widely used to promote the misconception that we as children of God are not *owners* of anything, but merely *stewards* of His creation.

Well, of course we are stewards, but we are *owners*, too, as Paul explains:

Everything belongs to you—whether Paul or Apollos or Peter, or the world, or life and death, or the present and the future. *Everything belongs to you, and you belong to Christ*, and Christ belongs to God   (1 Corinthians 3:21–23 NLT)

Do you see what great news this is? Look at the progression this way:

The earth is the Lord's, so everything belongs to Him.

But since *we* belong to Him, everything belongs to *us* as well!

This is all part of our blood covenant with Christ. When we acknowledge that everything we have belongs to Him, then the Bible teaches that everything He has belongs to us. That's a pretty amazing exchange, isn't it?

Authority to Sow and Reap

Although God gave humankind authority over His creation, He also put in place natural laws that govern how we must operate in order to be successful. One of these principles is the law of seedtime and harvest, which God said would never cease *"as long as the earth endures"* (Genesis 8:22).

Just as God ordained that we should exercise dominion over His creation, He also declared that our needs would be met as we sow and harvest seeds:

"Let the land produce vegetation: seed-bearing plants and trees on the land that bear fruit with seed in it, according to their various kinds." And it was so. The land produced vegetation: plants bearing seed according to their kinds and trees bearing fruit with seed in it according to their kinds. And God saw that it was good...."I give you every seed-bearing plant on the face of the whole earth and every tree that has fruit with seed in it. They will be yours for food."
(Genesis 1:11–12, 29 NIV)

By establishing seedtime and harvest, God gave humankind everything necessary to live abundantly and reign over the earth. Whenever we have a need, we can plant a seed and the harvest will come.

Be clear on this: *God is a good God!* He wants the best for us as His children, and His original creation had no sickness, poverty, strife, or death. In fact, here's how the creation was summarized: *"Then God saw everything that He had made, and indeed it was **very good**"* (Genesis 1:31).

Tending the Garden

We're told that Adam was given a specific assignment: *"Then the LORD God took the man and put him in the garden of Eden to tend and keep it"* (Genesis 2:15). Sometimes people get the misconception that this was just a small vegetable patch or backyard garden. But it was so much more than that.

Adam wasn't created to be a glorified weed-puller! Obviously not, since there weren't any weed problems until he sinned. Instead, Adam and Eve were given ownership and dominion over the garden. They were called to be in charge.

When Satan took the form of a serpent to beguile Eve, Adam had every right to confront him and throw him out of the garden. If Adam had been alert and willing to exercise his authority, he easily could have stopped the work of the enemy. But he abdicated his authority, and the devil came in and deceived his wife.

Death was not God's idea, but He had warned Adam, *"Of the tree of the knowledge of good and evil you shall not eat, for in the day that you eat of it you shall surely die"* (Genesis 2:17). Although Adam didn't physically die until he was 930 years old, he died spiritually as soon as he disobeyed the Lord.

How tragic that Adam and Eve squandered their God-given authority. The Lord had a great plan for them, but they forfeited it when they believed the devil instead of their Creator. After living in splendid abundance and even being entrusted with authority to name all the animals God created (see Genesis 2:19–20), Adam sunk so low that he ended up cultivating cursed ground, full of thorns and thistles (see Genesis 3:17–19).

How Much Authority Do We Have?

Once when Jeanne and I were visiting the Gulf Coast, the Lord gave me a helpful revelation of the power and authority we have as believers. As I was sitting on the beach, He began to speak to me, "Do you know why the waves only go so far and then stop?"

"Lord, they've been doing that for centuries," I replied.

"Yes, and it is because I told them it's as far as they could go!" God explained.

Although I was stunned by this at first, I found that the Bible says something very similar: *"He drew a circular horizon on the face of the waters, at the boundary of light and darkness"* (Job 26:10; see also Proverbs 8:29).

But I was troubled by the contrast between God's great power and the apparent powerlessness of many professing Christians. He helped me understand this by pointing me to John chapter 15. In this passage, Jesus begins with a reminder of how fruitful our lives can be when we abide in a vital union with Him, and how barren we'll be without this relationship:

> *I am the true vine, and My Father is the vinedresser. Every branch in Me that does not bear fruit He takes away; and every branch that bears fruit He prunes, that it may bear more fruit. You are already clean because of the word which I have spoken to you. Abide in Me, and I in you. As the branch cannot bear fruit of itself, unless it abides in the vine, neither can you, unless you abide in Me. I am the vine, you are the branches.* **He who abides in Me, and I in him, bears much fruit; for without Me you can do nothing.** (John 15:1–5)

It's so important that we grasp this two-sided principle: While we can *"do all things through Christ"* (Philippians 4:13) who gives us strength, apart from Him we can do nothing!

Our Power Through Abiding

Jesus goes on to give us a powerful statement about our authority in prayer:

> *If you abide in Me, and My words abide in you,* **you will ask what you desire, and it shall be done for you.** *By this My Father is glorified, that you bear much fruit; so you will be My disciples.* (John 15:7–8)

What amazing authority this is! If we are abiding in Christ and allowing His words to abide in us, whatever we ask in prayer will come to pass. After this promise becomes a reality for us, we will be able to speak to storms, waves, winds, and even hurricanes, and they will have to obey.

When I saw this, I asked the Lord, "You mean I could talk to a tsunami or ocean wave and tell it to go *backward?*"

He answered by pointing me back to what He said, "If you abide in Me and My words abide in you so much that you have a revelation of your authority, yes, you could actually overrule My natural laws."

Howard Carter, a minister during the early 1900s, had a revelation of this type of authority. As a conscientious objector during World War I, Carter was imprisoned. In his cell while he lay in bed, water leaked from the ceiling and dripped on his head. But through his study of the Bible, he had become convinced of his authority in Christ.

One day, Carter took the bold step of speaking to the dripping water, "I command you in the name of Jesus to reverse yourself and go the other way!" The water stopped dripping in his cell and actually went back up where it came from. It never dripped on him again.

My friend, you may not have a leaky ceiling to deal with, but surely there is *some* area of your life where you need to exercise your authority as a believer right now. Perhaps you're dealing with sickness in your own body or in a loved one's. Maybe the enemy has attacked your finances, and the bill collectors are harassing you every day. Or it could be that your home has been shaken by strained relationships.

Whatever situation you may be dealing with, it's time to believe God's promises and exercise the authority you have in the name of Jesus.

3

RECOGNIZING GOD'S COVENANT BLESSINGS

The mandate in Genesis 1:26–28 to *"be fruitful and multiply"* is not just referring to biological reproduction. As believers, we are called to reproduce spiritually, as well. Converts should be able to reproduce more converts, disciples should raise up additional disciples, and leaders should be equipping other leaders *"for the work of ministry"* (Ephesians 4:11–12).

This is an inherent part of God's original design, for *everything* in His creation is called to reproduce *"according to its kind"* (Genesis 1:11). And we will never fully understand the Great Commission until we first recognize this Old Testament principle of reproduction. It's significant that, when Jesus gave us the Great Commission in Matthew 28:18–20, He not only mentioned reproducing the number of disciples, but He started the passage with a statement of His *authority: "All authority has been given to Me in heaven and on earth"* (Matthew 28:18).

Do you see how this mirrors Genesis 1:26–28? The mandates in both places include *authority* as a necessary ingredient for success. This is rendered a variety of ways by different Bible translations:

+ *"have dominion"* (KJV, NKJV, ESV)

* "*rule*" (NASB, NIV)
* "*reign*" (NLT)
* "*have complete authority*" (AMP)

I particularly like how *The Message* paraphrases verse 28:

God blessed them: "Prosper! Reproduce! Fill Earth! Take charge! Be responsible for fish in the sea and birds in the air, for every living thing that moves on the face of Earth."

What an encouraging picture of God's intention for us as believers! He wants us to prosper, reproduce, fill the earth, take charge, and be responsible for everything He has made. And never forget: We will never be able to fulfill the *other* parts of our mandate unless we grasp the delegated authority God has given us to carry out that mandate.

Subduing Our Enemies

One of the reasons God has given us authority is to subdue our enemies so we can be fruitful and multiply. Because of God's covenant blessings, we can be *victors* instead of *victims*. We can overcome any foe that comes against us:

*You will chase your enemies, and they shall fall by the sword before you. Five of you shall chase a hundred, and a hundred of you shall put ten thousand to flight; your enemies shall fall by the sword before you. For I will look on you **favorably** and make you **fruitful, multiply you and confirm My covenant** with you.*
(Leviticus 26:7–9)

Notice that the victorious warfare described here is *supernatural* rather than natural. Because of God's blessing and favor, five of His children can defeat 100 of the enemy, and 100 of His children can defeat 10,000 of the enemy.

This provides a beautiful illustration of what Paul wrote about regarding our spiritual warfare as believers: "*We do not war according to the flesh. For the weapons of our warfare are not carnal but mighty in God for pulling down strongholds*" (2 Corinthians 10:3–4). And as the Lord told King Jehoshaphat, "*The battle is not yours, but God's*" (2 Chronicles 20:15).

This overwhelming victory is part of our blessings as God's covenant people. When we trust and obey Him, He gives us this sensational promise: *"I will be an enemy to your enemies and an adversary to your adversaries"* (Exodus 23:22). But victory over our enemies is only a small part of the benefits we have through our covenant with God:

> *I will make you **exceedingly fruitful**; and I will make nations of you, and kings shall come from you. And I will **establish My covenant** between Me and you and your **descendants** after you in their generations, for an **everlasting covenant**, to be God to you and your **descendants** after you. Also **I give to you and your descendants after you the land** in which you are a stranger, all the land of Canaan, as an everlasting possession; and **I will be their God**.*
>
> (Genesis 17:6–8)

Look at how exciting this is. When God is truly our God, He will make us not just a little bit fruitful but *"exceedingly fruitful."* He wants to multiply everything we have and everything we do, giving us His favor and increase. He wants to prosper us, give us land, and extend these amazing covenant blessings to all of our descendants. Wow! He is such a good God.

Family Blessings

If you have concerns today about your children or grandchildren, you need to see how your authority as a believer can extend God's covenant blessings to them. You see, the Lord doesn't want His blessings to stop with you or your generation—He wants to bless your entire family line, for many generations to come.

Hardly anything in this world is more powerful than the example set by a family that is displaying the Lord's covenant blessings, and it all starts when a parent *"fears the* LORD*"*:

> *Blessed is every one who fears the* LORD*, who walks in His ways. When you eat the labor of your hands, you shall be happy, and it shall be well with you. Your wife shall be like a fruitful vine in the very heart of your house, your children like olive plants all around your table. Behold, thus shall the man be blessed who fears the* LORD*. The* LORD *bless you out of Zion, and may you see the good*

of Jerusalem all the days of your life. Yes, may you see your children's children. Peace be upon Israel! (Psalm 128:1–6)

While a family that meets the psalmist's description may seem rare today, it was God's design from the beginning. He wanted families that reflected Him as our heavenly Father—godly parents and kids He could bless. In fact, just like a loving grandparent spoils their grandkids with excess, God wants to *lavish* His blessings on us! Look at these verses in *The Message*:

*Long, long ago he decided to adopt us into his family through Jesus Christ. (What pleasure he took in planning this!) He wanted us to enter into the **celebration of his lavish gift-giving** by the hand of his beloved Son.* (Ephesians 1:6)

*I ask...the God of our Master, Jesus Christ, the God of glory...to make you intelligent and discerning in knowing him personally, your eyes focused and clear, so that you can see exactly what it is he is calling you to do, grasp the immensity of this glorious way of life he has for his followers, oh, the **utter extravagance of his work in us who trust him**—endless energy, boundless strength!* (Ephesians 1:18–19)

*Now God has us where he wants us, with all the time in this world and the next to **shower grace and kindness** upon us in Christ Jesus.* (Ephesians 2:7)

Make no mistake about it, rather than being Scrooge-like and stingy, as some preachers portray our heavenly Father to be like, He is exceedingly generous and extravagant in His blessings.

Time to Review

From time to time, someone will tell me that they "tried" to exercise their authority and confront a certain issue in their life, but it just didn't seem to work. Inevitably, the problem turns out to be that they've left out some vital ingredient or condition. If that has been your experience as well, I encourage you to periodically review the main touchstones for success as a believer.

Here's a brief summary of some key points we've covered so far:

+ **What is God's purpose in delegating His authority to humankind?** For us to take dominion.

+ **Why is it important for us to take dominion?** Because it is a direct command from God. (See Genesis 1:26–28.)

+ **How can we take dominion?** The same way God created the universe—He spoke it into existence. (See Hebrews 11:3, 1:1–3.)

+ **How did Jesus say we can move the mountains in our lives?** Speak to them in faith. (See Matthew 17:20.)

+ **Conclusion: How can we take dominion?** We must take dominion with our words. Our words, like Jesus' words, are *"spirit, and they are life"* (John 6:33).

Remember that God is a covenantal God, and you can trust Him to keep His promises. Don't be shy or timid about making your needs known to Him! You should be *"bold as a lion"* (Proverbs 28:1) in exercising the authority you have in Jesus!

4

MANKIND: CROWNING GLORY OF CREATION

There's lots of talk about "self-image" and "self-esteem" in today's pop culture. And there is no doubt that every area of our life will be negatively impacted if we don't see ourselves correctly.

However, we will never gain the right perspective on who we are unless we start with what the Bible says about our creation and purpose. If we've been duped into believing that we're the descendants of ocean bacteria or monkeys, we'll never see ourselves as the magnificent creatures God designed us to be.

One day King David pondered humankind's role among all the other things God had made. He wondered about our rank and priority in the Lord's eyes:

When I consider Your heavens, the work of Your fingers, the moon and the stars, which You have ordained, what is man that You are mindful of him, and the son of man that You visit him? (Psalm 8:3–4)

This is a vital question for each of us to consider. Fortunately, David continued, giving us this powerful answer:

For You have made him a little lower than the angels, and You have crowned him with glory and honor. You have made him to have dominion over the works of Your hands; You have put all things under his feet.

(Psalm 8:5–6)

While we might be thrilled just to be *"a little lower than the angels,"* it's important to understand that the Hebrew word for *"angels"* is *elohim*—ordinarily translated as "God." Apparently, many of the translators have shied away from declaring this amazing truth: *God made humans a little lower than God Himself!* Yet an increasing number of Bible translations are now accurately translating *elohim* as "God." (These include the NASB, NLT, RSV, and ASV.)

If you are still clinging to the view that we are lower than the angels, look at this startling verse: *"Do you not know that we shall judge angels? How much more, things that pertain to this life?"* (1 Corinthians 6:3). Paul is saying here that rather than being created *lower* than angels, we actually will be their *judges* in eternity.

And here's how the writer of Hebrews describes angels: *"Are they not all ministering spirits sent forth to minister for those who will inherit salvation?"* (Hebrews 1:14). The calling of angels is to minister to *us* who will inherit salvation. Rather than being our masters, the angels are *"servant-spirits"* (Hebrews 1:14 NLT), sent out to care for us!

Why This Matters

Do you see the significance of David's statement that we were created *"a little lower than God"*? While the secular media and educational system promotes the idea that we are merely an evolved form of animals, the Bible describes a much grander heritage than that—a heritage that includes God's delegated authority over the rest of His creation.

You have made him to have dominion over the works of Your hands; You have put all things under his feet.   (Psalm 8:6)

This means we don't need to fear when storms or tornadoes come our way. We just need to use our authority as believers! We may need to speak to the weather, dispatch an angel, apply our blood-covenant privileges, or take some other action that the Holy Spirit directs. But we can confidently exercise our authority in Jesus' name, standing on God's promises to protect our own homes and communities.

When I got this revelation, I changed the way I spoke to the elements during stormy times. Now I say, "Lord, I am taking my place as Your authority on earth, and I am standing in the gap like Abraham did for Sodom and Gomorrah. As I stand in this place as Your delegated authority, I come against perverted weather patterns that would try to steal, kill, or destroy the blessings You intend for Your people."

I am not responsible for *everyone's* neighborhood or house, but God has given me authority to protect my own. Everyone has their own sphere of responsibility, and they must act with their God-given authority to protect what has been entrusted to them. When we understand this, we won't have to hide in our basements in fear of the storms; we can rebuke them as Jesus demonstrated. (See Luke 8:22–25.) The elements have no choice but to obey us, since we've received God's delegated authority over the earth. Understanding this can save our lives.

Is Something Still Missing?

Hebrews 2:6–9 quotes David's words in Psalm 8 about the awesome calling of humankind to exercise God's authority over the earth, but then it continues with this explanation: *"For in that He put **all** in subjection under him [mankind], He left **nothing that is not put under him**. But now we do not yet see all things put under him. But we see Jesus"* (Hebrews 2:8–9).

This passage explains quite a bit. First, it reaffirms God's intention that *everything* would be put under the authority He has delegated to humankind. It goes on to say that *nothing* in God's creation has been excluded from this.

However, the passage also raises a vital question: If indeed we have dominion over everything God has made, why don't we always *see* that played out in the world around us? Although the writer of Hebrews admits we don't fully see humanity exercising this authority, he adds this powerful line: ***"But we see Jesus."*** God is *"bringing many sons to glory"* (Hebrews 2:10)—you and me!—and Jesus is our perfect forerunner. He already is seated at the Father's right hand, endowed with absolute authority over creation. (See Hebrews 1:3.)

So here's a summary of what the Bible teaches about man's authority:

+ As part of the original creation, God gave humankind complete authority to rule over the earth and all it contains.

+ When Adam and Eve sinned in Genesis chapter 3, their authority was perverted and limited because they had allowed Satan to influence them.

+ By His death on the cross and His resurrection, Jesus won back *"all authority"* (Matthew 28:18) to rule over the earth.

+ Despite what Jesus did in winning back humankind's authority, most people— even most Christians—are oblivious to the authority that is rightfully theirs. Thus, they don't yet see humankind experiencing its intended authority over the earth.

+ However, as Hebrews 2:9 points out, *"We see Jesus."* This means that, as the perfect Man, Jesus has been exalted far above all rule and authority, including any of the devil's minions.

+ Since we are seated with Christ in heavenly realms, we've been restored to a position of authority over the earth. Yet we experience this authority only when we choose to believe it and exercise it.

The Spirit Without Measure

Jesus was endued with unlimited power, described as having *"the Spirit without measure"* (John 3:34 NASB). This is rendered in the *New Living Translation*, *"For he is sent by God. He speaks God's words, for God gives him the Spirit without limit."*

Likewise, the body of Christ has been given the Spirit without measure, for Paul describes it as *"the fullness of Him who fills all in all"* (Ephesians 1:23). We are *"being built together for a dwelling place of God in the Spirit"* (Ephesians 2:22), with His ultimate goal that we *"may be filled with all the fullness of God"* (Ephesians 3:19).

However, *individually*, we've been given the Holy Spirit *with* measure. Only when we are joined together *"will all the saints"* can we comprehend *"what is the width and length and depth and height—to know the love of Christ which passes knowledge"* (Ephesians 3:18–19).

Unfortunately, though, the body of Christ has been weakened by ignorance and unbelief concerning the power and authority available to it. Many of us Christians have the misconception that God alone has authority, and we are just strangers, pilgrims, and beggars. Although we have overwhelming authority through our union with Christ, many churches have taught that we have no authority at all.

Years ago, a salesman who used to call on our church handed me an essay he thought I would like to read. He said, "Our pastor and ministry staff did a study on whether the baptism and gifts of the Holy Spirit are relevant for today."

"And what was their conclusion?" I asked.

He told me they had determined that the supernatural gifts of the Holy Spirit were not available or needed anymore.

I gave him his paper back. Although he was disappointed, I didn't want to read it. I told him politely, "I've already read *God's* paper, the Bible, and it says the power of the Holy Spirit is available to us today."

Isn't it amazing how people come up with their own ideas and theories about what is true? We must stick with what God's Word really says! This sometimes tests our faith. If a doctor diagnoses someone with a terrible disease that has no medical cure, will we stand on the Word and declare that we are healed by the stripes Jesus bore for us? (See 1 Peter 2:24.) We must know what God has promised, believe it, and then stand on our authority as believers.

5

PARADISE LOST—AND FOUND

God had wonderful plans for humankind. He declared that Adam and Eve and everything else He created were *"very good"* (Genesis 1:31). The first man and woman were lovingly placed in a garden filled with overwhelming abundance. What a marvelous start!

But everything began to unravel when Adam and Eve disobeyed God and fell from their lofty position in His creation. Their authority was relinquished when they rebelled against His command and allowed sin to enter the world. This changed everything. Death entered in the human race and mankind could no longer live in the beautiful garden of abundance where God had placed them.

We are still experiencing the consequences of the Fall in our world today. Although we were created to live in lavish beauty of the garden of Eden, instead we find ourselves in a fallen world. This has been an agonizing turn of events, not just for humankind, but for the entire creation:

We know that the whole creation groans and labors with birth pangs together until now. Not only that, but we also who have the firstfruits of the Spirit, even we ourselves groan within ourselves, eagerly waiting for the adoption, the redemption of our body. (Romans 8:22–23)

Still today, the earth is groaning. All over the globe, many types of natural disasters are occurring—even though there's nothing "natural" about them. As believers, we have authority over what the world calls natural disasters. They're actually not natural at all, in the sense that they are part of God's original intent in creation. Instead of being called natural disasters, they should be called *demonic* disasters.

When Adam and Eve relinquished their authority, Satan was allowed to pervert the way of nature. Just as this wicked fallen archangel attacks humankind in order to steal, kill, and destroy, he also delights in destroying the earth. All this is because *"through one man sin entered the world, and death through sin, and thus death spread to all men, because all sinned"* (Romans 5:12). It only took one man to bring sin into the world, but ultimately we *all* have sinned. (See Romans 3:23.)

The First Man and the Last Adam

Except for Jesus, everyone born after Adam has been born spiritually dead, separated from God. Because of Adam's sin, death reigned until Jesus came and reversed the curse for those who believe:

> And so it is written, "The first man Adam became a living being." The last Adam became a life-giving spirit. However, the spiritual is not first, but the natural, and afterward the spiritual. The first man was of the earth, made of dust; the second Man is the Lord from heaven. As was the man of dust, so also are those who are made of dust; and as is the heavenly Man, so also are those who are heavenly. And as we have borne the image of the man of dust, we shall also bear the image of the heavenly Man.   (1 Corinthians 15:45–49)

Adam is called *"the first man,"* the beginning of the human race. In contrast, the Bible refers to Jesus as *"the last Adam,"* He's *not* called "the *second* Adam," because that would leave room for a third or fourth or fifth. Jesus secured our redemption as the last and final Adam. Adam was the originator of the fallen line of humanity, but Jesus was the beginning of the new creation. And as the last Adam, Jesus paid the price for our redemption and originated the final line of humankind:

> For if by the one man's offense death reigned through the one, much more those who receive abundance of grace and of the gift of righteousness will reign in life through the One, Jesus Christ. Therefore, as through one man's offense judgment

came to all men, resulting in condemnation, even so through one Man's righteous act the free gift came to all men, resulting in justification of life.

(Romans 5:17–18)

The Gift of Righteousness

God's righteousness is a free gift. Jesus paid for it with His life, but it is free to us. Because of Adam's disobedience, we are all born sinners. However, we have now been made the righteousness of God in Christ. (See 2 Corinthians 5:21.)

God gave us the Law of Moses to show us right from wrong. It was like a stop sign at an intersection. If there is no stop sign, we don't know we are supposed to stop, and we are likely to drive right through the intersection without stopping. It's technically not wrong, because there is no law. But when there's a stop sign and we drive through the intersection without stopping, we know it is wrong, and we have broken the law. That is what the Law of Moses did. It said, "Don't go there" and "Don't do that."

Because of the Law, Paul was able to clearly see the fallen nature of mankind, separated from God:

For I know that in me (that is, in my flesh) nothing good dwells; for to will is present with me, but how to perform what is good I do not find. For the good that I will to do, I do not do; but the evil I will not to do, that I practice. Now if I do what I will not to do, it is no longer I who do it, but sin that dwells in me.

(Romans 7:18–20)

Moreover the law entered that the offense might abound. But where sin abounded, grace abounded much more, so that as sin reigned in death, even so grace might reign through righteousness to eternal life through Jesus Christ our Lord.

(Romans 5:20–21)

Having become the righteousness of God in Christ, our authority has been regained. In fact, as believers in Christ, we have just as much a right to exercise authority on earth today as Adam did when God created him in the garden.

Yes, it's still true that *"your adversary the devil walks about like a roaring lion, seeking whom he may devour"* (1 Peter 5:8). But the devil's power is no match for the victory Jesus obtained for you on the cross. Never forget that Jesus' victory on the cross is far greater than Adam's sin in the garden.

Redeemed from the Curse

As a result of Adam and Eve's fall in Genesis 3, humankind and the earth itself were cursed. Instead of enjoying unbroken fellowship with God and the lavish abundance of the garden of Eden, Adam was told,

> Cursed is the ground for your sake; in toil you shall eat of it all the days of your life. Both thorns and thistles it shall bring forth for you, and you shall eat the herb of the field. In the sweat of your face you shall eat bread till you return to the ground. (Genesis 3:17–19)

Prior to this, there had been no sickness, anxiety, broken relationships, poverty, or death. But everything was disrupted when the curse came.

Thankfully, Jesus' death and resurrection broke the power of the curse over those who believe. He redeemed us from the curse by becoming a curse for us:

> Christ has redeemed us from the curse of the law, having become a curse for us (for it is written, "Cursed is everyone who hangs on a tree"), that the blessing of Abraham might come upon the Gentiles in Christ Jesus, that we might receive the promise of the Spirit through faith. (Galatians 3:13–14)

Do you see how significant this is? Jesus completely reversed the curse. Instead of living from hand to mouth, trying to make a living by the sweat of our brow, we are free to enjoy God's abundant provision once again. And when Satan tries to harass us with sickness or strife, we can boldly declare in Jesus' name, "The curse is broken! None of those negative things have a right to torment me anymore."

If you want to see the stark contrast between a life of blessing and a life under the curse, I encourage you to read Deuteronomy 28. Instead of disease, defeat, and lack, God promises an amazing life of blessing and fruitfulness when we *"diligently obey the voice of the LORD"* (Deuteronomy 28:1).

Paul wrote that Christ broke the curse so that *"the blessing of Abraham might come upon the Gentiles in Christ Jesus"* (Galatians 3:13–14). We are no longer under the curse of the law; we are *"Abraham's seed, and heirs according to the promise"* (Galatians

3:29). Just as God told Abraham, He promises us today: *"I will bless you...and you shall **be** a blessing"* (Genesis 12:2). What a wonderful life this can be!

6

JOB, MAN OF AUTHORITY

Job was an example of a man blessed by God, given great authority on the earth. Contrary to what most of us have been taught, the primary message of his story is not one of suffering, but of faith. Yes, Job did suffer—and suffer greatly—for about nine months. But for most of his life, he was blessed with abundance and favor. He was an overcomer, and his story is all about faith, dominion, and a believer's authority.

The Bible describes Job as a man who *"was blameless and upright, and one who feared God and shunned evil"* (Job 1:1). He had numerous children and extravagant wealth, to the extent that he was *"the greatest of all the people of the East"* (verse 3). Even today, if you had seven thousand sheep, three thousand camels, five hundred oxen and donkeys, and a large household of servants, you would be considered very rich.

Satan had to acknowledge that Job had been greatly blessed with God's provision and protection. He said to the Lord, *"Have You not made a hedge around him, around his household, and around all that he has on every side? You have blessed the work of his hands, and his possessions have increased in the land"* (Job 1:10).

Yet Satan had a theory about what would happen if Job was tested and no longer had his great possessions to rely upon. He told God, *"Stretch out Your hand and touch all that he has, and he will surely curse You to Your face!"* (Job 1:11).

A common misunderstanding of the first chapter of Job is that God actually invited Satan to attack Job. I don't believe that. In addition, we have to be careful about accepting as truth everything Job said about God. For example, shortly after his trials began, Job said, *"Naked I came from my mother's womb, and naked shall I return there. The LORD gave, and the LORD has taken away; blessed be the name of the LORD"* (Job 1:21). There's even a popular Christian song today that echoes this misconception that the Lord "gives and takes away."

But I challenge you to find any passage of Scripture that says our heavenly Father randomly takes things away from people who are walking in a loving, obedient relationship with Him. Sure, He may remove or prune things from our lives if they are hindering us from bearing fruit. (See John 15:1–5.) And yes, there are some things that happen in this life that we won't fully understand until we get heaven. Yet Job's statement makes it sound like God delights in giving us things and then taking them away from us. Nothing could be further from the truth! Yet many Christians have adopted this as their view of God.

Fatalism and God's Sovereignty

As Job's trials were underway, his wife gave him this unwelcomed piece of advice: *"Do you still hold fast to your integrity? Curse God and die!"* (Job 2:9). What a discouraging outlook. When we are going through difficult times, it is so important to listen to those who speak words of faith to us instead of words of unbelief.

Job realized his wife was speaking *"as one of the foolish women speaks"* (Job 2:10). But then he makes a misguided statement of his own: *"Shall we indeed accept good from God, and shall we not accept adversity?"* (Job 2:10).

Job and his wife had a perspective that is still very common today. They looked at Job's situation and concluded that he certainly would die before long—and his wife said he might as well get it over with! Both of them were embracing *fatalism*— the view that the outcome of our lives is predetermined, and that there's nothing we can do to change it.

Fatalism says that the events in your life are inevitable; so you should just accept them and get over it. You have no real responsibility for how your life will turn out. Everything is predetermined by God, and you never know what He is going to do. There's nothing you can do to change your future, because God does whatever He wants to do.

The fatalistic outlook of Job and his wife was compounded by their distorted view that God gives with one hand and takes away with the other. The Lord does whatever He wants to do, whenever and however He wants to do it, because He is sovereign. Job was so extreme in this view that he even said, *"Though He slay me, yet will I trust Him"* (Job 13:15). Although Job was well-intentioned in this view, he was totally wrong in his perception of the Lord. *God* wasn't the one trying to slay him; *Satan* was! (See John 10:10, if you don't believe me.)

Job and his wife were not alone in their misconceptions. Even today, many Christians believe this same way, and it cripples them from exercising their authority as believers. Feeling like helpless victims of fate, they have no hope of improving their circumstances.

God Is a Good God

God is good—and He's good *all the time.* We learn this from the very first chapter of the Bible: *"God saw everything that He had made, and indeed it was very good"* (Genesis 1:31). Not just *some* things were good, but *"everything"* God made was good—even *"very good."*

That's why James told us, *"Do not be deceived, my beloved brethren.* **Every good thing given and every perfect gift is from above**, *coming down from the Father of lights, with whom there is no variation or shifting shadow"* (James 1:16–17 NASB). You see, we're deceived if we fail to understand that our heavenly Father loves us and wants to give us good gifts. (See Matthew 7:7–11.) And there's *"no variation"* in how He acts toward His people.

So where did evil come from? Although God didn't create evil, He did create choice. Lucifer chose to rebel against God, and that set in motion a ripple effect of evil that eventually engulfed Adam and Eve and the entire world.

Job was a righteous man, but God rebuked him for misrepresenting Him:

God addressed Job next from the eye of the storm, and this is what he said: "I have some more questions for you, and I want straight answers. Do you presume to tell me what I'm doing wrong? Are you calling me a sinner so you can be a saint?" (Job 40:6–8 MSG)

By portraying God as the creator of evil and distress, Job was spreading a tragic misconception. This did not make the Lord happy, and He let Job know it. In essence, by blaming God for his troubles, Job tried to vindicate himself. The *New King James Version* of verse 8 puts God's question this way: *"Would you condemn Me that you may be justified?"* Meanwhile, as God is being wrongfully accused, Satan—the true author of Job's calamities—is being let off the hook.

Don't Believe the Lie

If you let it, a fatalistic mind-set will cripple the use of your authority as a believer. By believing the misconception that God is in total control, you can justify yourself and shirk all responsibility for the circumstances of your life. If you blame God for everything that is happening to you, you're portraying yourself as completely innocent!

The lie of fatalism will keep you from rebuking a tornado or hurricane—because it's sent by God, after all. Who are *you* to stand against God's sovereignty? The same logic will keep you from opposing cancer, poverty, or rebellion in your kids. You'll assume that every attack is part of God's sovereign will and that it would be futile to resist!

Fatalism wraps itself in a religious spirit, but it violates everything the Bible says about our heavenly Father. Christians who adopt this perspective always end up powerless and ineffective. They have undercut their ability to exercise authority and change their circumstances.

Judging God as Faithful

While fatalism judges God as unpredictable and fickle, the Scriptures testify that He is faithful and reliable. Job was reprimanded by the Lord for misjudging Him, but the secret of many biblical heroes is that they judged Him *correctly.* Let me explain.

Abraham *"believed in the LORD, and He accounted it to him for righteousness"* (Genesis 15:6). Likewise, his wife, Sarah, determined that God was worthy of her faith: *"By faith Sarah herself also received strength to conceive seed, and she bore a child when she was past the age, because **she judged Him faithful who had promised"*** (Hebrews 11:11).

What a contrast. Job chose to judge God and blame Him, but Sarah judged God as faithful. Those who embrace fatalism and follow in Job's steps will always be hindered by nagging questions like, "Why did God let this happen?" or "Why did He do this?" or "Why did He allow the devil to do this to me?" They will never be able to totally trust the Lord and stand on His Word. With a fatalistic worldview, they won't be able to grasp the awesome delegated authority and power He has given to humankind.

If you haven't been judging God as faithful, it's time to have your mind renewed so you can believe the truth. At the end of Job's story, he finally realized his erroneous thinking:

> Then Job replied to the Lord: "I know that you can do anything, and no one can stop you. You asked, 'Who is this that questions my wisdom with such ignorance?' It is I—and I was talking about things I knew nothing about, things far too wonderful for me. You said, 'Listen and I will speak! I have some questions for you, and you must answer them.' I had only heard about you before, but now I have seen you with my own eyes. I take back everything I said, and I sit in dust and ashes to show my repentance." (Job 42:1–6 NLT)

In order to exercise your authority as a believer, it is absolutely essential that you see the Lord correctly. Perhaps, as you read this book, you realize that your view of God has been twisted over the years. If so, embrace the truth of Scripture and do as Job did—*repent!*

My friend, when you receive a revelation of who God really is and who you are in Him, your turnaround can come amazingly fast, as it did for Job:

> The LORD restored Job's losses when he prayed for his friends. Indeed the LORD gave Job twice as much as he had before....Now the LORD blessed the latter days of Job more than his beginning. (Job 42:10, 12)

This can be the happy ending of *your* story, too!

7

A BELIEVER...IN *WHAT*?

You've probably met people who say they are believers, but they are defeated, sick, and broken. Yes, they believe in Jesus and have been given eternal life, but that seems to be the full extent of their faith. Although they may believe in being born again through faith, they don't believe in prosperity...or deliverance...or healing—which are just as scriptural as the gospel of salvation.

Whatever we receive from God comes on the basis of faith. That's just how He's set things up. Paul wrote to Timothy about *"God's provision which is by faith"* (1 Timothy 1:4 NASB).

Every born-again Christian understands that forgiveness comes on the basis of faith. We quote verses like these:

God so loved the world that He gave His only begotten Son, that whoever believes in Him should not perish but have everlasting life. (John 3:16)

To Him all the prophets witness that, through His name, whoever believes in Him will receive remission of sins. (Acts 10:43)

Just as eternal life and forgiveness of sins are given to us when we *believe*, we must activate and receive God's other promises in the same way. We are born again when we believe Jesus is the Christ and receive His forgiveness. But God has so much more in store for us than that!

I've concluded that there are different kinds of "believers"—those who seek to believe *all* of God's promises, those who stop believing His promises at their initial salvation, and those who pick and choose which promises to believe.

So what kind of believer are *you*? Have you been content to believe only for a "ticket to heaven," or do you believe *all* the promises of the Word of God? Have you been guilty of treating the Scriptures as a cafeteria, where you can pick and choose which promises you will believe and appropriate for your life?

If you're truly a Christian, you believe that Jesus Christ is the Son of God, that He died for your sins, and that God raised Him from the dead. Because you've acted on your faith by receiving Christ as your Savior, you've received the gift of eternal life, and you've been made righteous in Him. As Paul wrote, *"Having been justified by faith, we have peace with God through our Lord Jesus Christ"* (Romans 5:1).

Your salvation isn't a matter of *chance*, it's a matter of *choice*: Your decision to accept God's offer of eternal life in His Son. When you receive Him, you are given *authority* to enter God's family: *"To as many as did receive and welcome Him, He gave the **authority** (power, privilege, right) to become the children of God, that is, to those who believe in (adhere to, trust in, and rely on) His name"* (John 1:12 AMP).

So far, so good. But God wants you to believe the *rest* of His promises, too. Your authority as a believer includes a lot more than just having the right to be a child of God and go to heaven when you die!

Lessons from Abraham

The first step to growing in your spiritual authority as a believer is to put your full faith in the trustworthiness of God. James 2:23 quotes Genesis 15:6 concerning the life of Abraham, the father of our faith: *"**Abraham believed God**, and it was accounted to him for righteousness."* Abraham didn't just believe facts *about* God, he *"believed God."* He had a covenant relationship with the Lord, and the relationship was based upon complete trust. We're told that Abraham's faith was proven to be genuine when *"he offered Isaac his son on the altar"* (James 2:21).

But not everyone's profession of faith is this sincere or genuine. One day, Jesus encountered some Jewish people who professed to believe in Him. He told them, *"If you abide in My word, you are My disciples indeed. And you shall know the truth, and the truth shall make you free"* (John 8:31–32).

However, it soon became clear that these professing followers were believing in Abraham more than they were believing in Jesus: *"We are Abraham's descendants, and have never been in bondage to anyone. How can you say, 'You will be made free'?"* (John 8:33).

Friend, everyone believes in *something*. But some beliefs, though they may be well-meaning, are totally amiss. These Jews were basing their salvation on allegiance to Abraham and their Jewish heritage, and Jesus told them how erroneous this was: *"I know that you are Abraham's descendants, but you seek to kill Me, because My word has no place in you"* (John 8:37).

Yes, these people were physically descended from Abraham, and they delighted in saying, *"Abraham is our father"* (John 8:39). But Jesus challenged them that their deeds were diametrically opposed to the example set by Abraham: *"If you were Abraham's children, you would do the works of Abraham. But now you seek to kill Me, a Man who has told you the truth which I heard from God. Abraham did not do this. You do the deeds of your father"* (John 8:39–41).

At this point, the Jewish people changed their story and claimed that *God* was their father. Yet Jesus pointed out that, like their previous claim that Abraham was their father, the new argument was just as hypocritical: *"If God were your Father, you would love Me, for I proceeded forth and came from God; nor have I come of Myself, but He sent Me"* (John 8:42).

Finally, the truth came out. Instead of having Abraham or God as their father, these people were told by Jesus, *"You are of your father the devil"* (John 8:44).

You see, it's not enough to be a "believer"—we must believe the *right things*! The people Jesus was talking with in this story had all kinds of wild beliefs that were not rooted in reality or demonstrated in their lives. Many people today are suffering from the same kinds of illusions about faith. Some are basing their hopes on their family's Christian heritage instead of having a personal relationship with Christ. Others believe the fallacy that *everyone* is "a child of God," when the Bible clearly teaches otherwise.

True freedom and victory come only when we *"know the truth"* (John 8:32). This means that we study, meditate upon, and apply God's Word as the basis of our beliefs.

Believing the Whole Gospel

Understand this: You have to believe *all* the gospel if you're going to exercise *all* authority. You can't just believe certain parts of it. The same Scripture passage in Isaiah 53 that says, *"He was wounded for our transgressions, He was bruised for our iniquities"* (Isaiah 53:5) *also* says that He has…

- *"borne our griefs"* (verse 4)
- *"carried our sorrows"* (verse 4)
- been chastised *"for our peace"* (verse 5)
- paid for our healing, because *"by His stripes we are healed"* (verse 5)

Forgiveness of sins is certainly not the only "benefit" God gives to us in Christ:

Bless the LORD, *O my soul, and forget not all* **His benefits***: who* **forgives** *all your iniquities, who* **heals** *all your diseases, who* **redeems** *your life from destruction, who* **crowns** *you with lovingkindness and tender mercies, who* **satisfies** *your mouth with good things, so that your* **youth is renewed** *like the eagle's.*

(Psalm 103:2–5)

Friend, as you consider the wide array of God's promises, have you been guilty of picking and choosing which ones you will believe? As we're reminded in Ephesians 3:20, *"God can do anything, you know—far more than you could ever imagine or guess or request in your wildest dreams!"* (MSG). So if you are struggling to exercise faith and authority in a certain area, at least take time to find someone who believes the part you're missing. Allow them to take authority on your behalf during your time of need.

Don't Be Double-Minded!

Just as there are "unbelieving believers"—who refuse to accept and appropriate many of the Bible's promises—there also are many double-minded believers. Although these people believe all the right things, they doubt their beliefs and vacillate on whether or not they will trust God.

For example, James wrote, *"If any of you lacks wisdom, let him ask of God, who gives to all liberally and without reproach, and it will be given to him. But let him ask in faith, **with no doubting**"* (James 1:5–6). James then goes on to describe the tragic consequences reaped by a person who is double-minded:

> *He who doubts is like a wave of the sea driven and tossed by the wind. For let not that man suppose that he will receive anything from the Lord; he is a double-minded man, unstable in all his ways.* (James 1:5–8)

Hopefully this doesn't describe you, my friend. God forbid that you would be *"like a wave of the sea driven and tossed by the wind."* A double-minded person is *"unstable in all his ways"* and can't expect to *"receive anything from the Lord."*

This aligns perfectly with what Jesus teaches us about mountain-moving faith:

> *Assuredly, I say to you, whoever says to this mountain, "Be removed and be cast into the sea," **and does not doubt in his heart**, but believes that those things he says will be done, **he will have whatever he says.*** (Mark 11:23)

Why would a person pray a bold prayer or speak to a "mountain" in audacious faith, only to negate their efforts by doubting in their heart? Yet this is a common occurrence! All the while, God tells us we can have "whatever we say"; but we must not allow unbelief to undercut our miracle.

You see, God has given us authority to do mighty miracles, but unbelief can hinder us from *standing* in that authority. So let's cast double-mindedness aside, crying out to God as King David did:

> *Teach me your way, LORD, that I may **rely on your faithfulness; give me an undivided heart**, that I may fear your name.* (Psalm 86:11 NIV)

Yes, Lord, we want to rely on Your faithfulness. Give us undivided hearts!

8

UNDERSTANDING
AUTHORITY AND POWER

W. E. Gladstone was the Prime Minister of Great Britain when Queen Victoria was on the throne. Part of his job as Prime Minister was to bring legislation from Parliament to the queen for her to sign. Without the queen's signature, the legislation wouldn't become law, and it would have no bearing on people's lives.

On one occasion, when Gladstone presented a piece of legislation to Queen Victoria for her to sign, she read it and then put down her pen, saying, "I do not agree with this, and I am not going to sign it."

He replied, "But Madame, you *must* sign this law."

She looked at him and responded, "*I* am the Queen of England."

"Mum," Gladstone declared, "*I* am the people of England."

Finally persuaded by his boldness, the queen reluctantly signed the law. Why? Because the people of England had given W. E. Gladstone *authority* to act on their behalf. When he spoke or took action as Prime Minister, he did so "in the name" of the English people.

You see, the authority we have is *delegated* authority, gained as we submit to an authority higher than our own. We each have a certain "sphere" of authority in the earthly realm, but only Jesus can say, "*All authority has been given to Me in heaven and on earth*" (Matthew 28:18). As believers, *our* authority is derived from *His* authority.

Authority and *power* have some parallels to each other, but they are two entirely different things. If a police officer is standing in the street, all he has to do is raise his hand and a whole line of cars will stop. Although the officer doesn't have the *power* to halt the tons of metal propelled in his direction by powerful gasoline engines, he does have the *authority* to require them to stop. People stop because they recognize the officer's authority, not because he is stronger or more powerful than their cars.

A burglar does not have authorization or authority to break into someone's home, but he does have the power to do so. If a police officer is called to the scene in time, he has authority to arrest the thief. And the officer's authority trumps the thief's power. Why? Because the authority of the officer has been delegated to him from the government and its citizens.

Utilizing the Spirit's Power

A believer has been given both authority and power. Through the Holy Spirit, we've been given "*power from on high*" (Luke 24:49). In the mighty name of Jesus, we can "*cast out demons…speak with new tongues…lay hands on the sick, and they will recover*" (Mark 16:17–18). Sadly, though, many believers don't realize the amazing power available to them.

I have a friend who bought his first smart phone a few months ago. When I asked him how he liked it, he surprised me by saying, "Well, Happy, I can't tell much difference between this and the phone I had before."

"You must be kidding!" I responded. "What kinds of things are you doing on your new phone?"

"Oh, I just use it like any other phone—to call people and occasionally send a text message."

I could hardly believe my ears. My friend had purchased an expensive phone and data plan, but he was using only a very small percentage of its potential. The phone *could have* awakened him in the morning, given him the weather report, reminded him of his schedule for the day, provided him navigation to his appointments, kept track of his finances, surfed the Internet, checked his e-mails, told him the best restaurants in the area, read the Bible to him, taken pictures of his grandkids…and so much more!

What a fitting illustration of how little we utilize the power of God's Spirit in our lives. Some of this is a result of ignorance. My friend probably had no idea all the features available to him in his new phone. In addition to our ignorance of the power and authority given to us as believers, I think we also suffer from *spiritual laziness* at times, unwilling to take the time to learn how to use what God has provided us with. The owner of a fancy new smart phone has incredible power at his or her fingertips—but it will be squandered unless he or she downloads the apps and puts it to work.

Deciding to Believe

I've always been intrigued by the response of Paul's audience when they listened to him as he *"explained and solemnly testified about the kingdom of God, persuading them concerning Jesus from both the Law of Moses and the Prophets, from morning till evening"* (Acts 28:22–23). I'm sure Paul gave a powerful presentation of the gospel, but that didn't mean everyone was convinced: *"**Some believed** the things which were spoken, and **some believed not**"* (verse 24 kjv).

"Some believed"; "some believed not." But in reality, even those who *"believed not"* were believing in something. You see, even though some people say they don't believe in anything, they really do. They may believe in God, themselves, a tree, a pebble, little green aliens, or even clouds, but they believe in something.

People either believe there is a God, or they believe there isn't a God. They either believe Jesus is the Son of God, or they believe He isn't. They either believe that healing and other gifts of the Holy Spirit are available to us today, or they believe those things are no longer available. Everyone believes something, regardless of whether that "something" is true or not.

When confronted with the truth Paul presented to them, *"some believed not."* It doesn't say they believed nothing. They just chose to believe something other than the truth Paul shared from the Scriptures.

Perhaps you've never really considered faith to be a choice; but it is. *The Message* paraphrases Acts 28:24 this way: *"Some of them were persuaded by what he said, but others **refused to believe** a word of it."* These people had a choice to make, and they chose *not* to believe!

Friend, each of us has to make a similar choice. Will we choose to believe God's Word, or will we refuse? In Deuteronomy 30:19–20, Moses set this kind of choice before Israel:

> I call heaven and earth as witnesses today against you, that I have set before you life and death, blessing and cursing; therefore choose life, that both you and your descendants may live; that you may love the LORD your God, that you may obey His voice, and that you may cling to Him, for He is your life and the length of your days; and that you may dwell in the land which the LORD swore to your fathers, to Abraham, Isaac, and Jacob, to give them.

This is just one of many biblical examples where God's people had to decide whether or not to *believe* and *obey* His voice. It is the same choice we face as believers today. If we believe and obey the Lord, we will reap a life of abundance and blessings. But if we don't believe and obey, the unfortunate result will be curses and death.

Faith Enables Submission

Without understanding faith, you cannot submit to authority. The carnal nature will rise up and rebel against submission unless you've first learned to entrust yourself to God. The reason Jesus had no trouble submitting to authority or walking the path to Calvary was because He had total trust in the Father's love and wisdom.

Jesus gave an intriguing reply to the disciples when they asked Him to increase their faith:

> If you have faith as a mustard seed, you can say to this mulberry tree, "Be pulled up by the roots and be planted in the sea," and it would obey you. And which of you, having a servant plowing or tending sheep, will say to him when he has come in from the field, "Come at once and sit down to eat"? But will he not rather say to him, "Prepare something for my supper, and gird yourself and serve me till I have eaten and drunk, and afterward you will eat and drink"? Does he think that servant because he did the things that were commanded him? I think not. So likewise you, when you have done all those things which you are commanded, say, "We are unprofitable servants. We have done what was our duty to do."
>
> (Luke 17:5–10)

The point often missed in Jesus' story here is that *faith is a servant*. Instead of having a mind of its own, faith's job is to serve us. When *we* submit ourselves to God and His delegated authorities, faith is required to submit to *us*!

We know from James 4:7 that if we've submitted our lives to God, we can resist the devil, and he must flee from us. But what if we are *not* submitted to God? Then the devil isn't obligated to flee! And he can *tell* whether or not we're truly living in submission to God by our actions, words, and character.

Fulfilling Our Assignments

Submission to God is a matter of *obedience*, both to His written Word and to the specific assignments He gives us. Sometimes His assignments are small and seemingly insignificant, and other times they may seem rather overwhelming. In either case, we must "trust and obey" if we expect to walk in God's authority.

Several times now, the Lord has told me very clearly that I was supposed to write a book. I'm not particularly gifted as a writer, so it has sometimes been tempting to procrastinate and delay.

"Lord, let someone else write a book on that topic!" I've protested at times. But God simply replies, "If I wanted someone else to write the book, why would I have told *you* to do it?"

Friend, believe me on this: Delayed obedience is disobedience, and procrastination is just another form of rebellion.

When Andrew Wommack asked me to teach the third-year students in Charis Bible College a few years ago, I was hesitant at first. Although I was honored by the invitation, I thought, *Why would he ask me? There are better pastors, bigger churches, and people with deeper revelations.* Yet God wanted me to put everything I've experienced in more than thirty years of pastoral ministry into a syllabus. It wasn't my idea at all. You might say He forced me to do it.

That reminded me of an experience back in my high school days. My English teacher wrote in my yearbook, "Happy, you can do anything, if you have to do it!"

One night I was visiting with my friend Eddie Miller, founder of the Country and Western Music Academy in Hollywood, and cofounder of the Nashville Songwriters Association International. When I asked him how he wrote his songs, his answer shocked me. "I force myself to write them," he said. He explained that he booked studio sessions and scheduled all the recording artists, musicians, and audio engineers before he wrote his songs. He did this because he knew that the deadline would force him to have the songs ready in time.

And sometimes God will require you to do something simply because He wants you to do it. It isn't because of your expert knowledge. Rather, it's because He's training and developing you for something He's planning for your future.

Perhaps there was a time when God asked you to work in a certain ministry of the church, but you didn't want to submit to the authority involved in that assignment. So you hesitated, all because you had a problem with authority. You wanted to come when you wanted, leave when you wanted, and do what you wanted. But God is trying to mature you and teach you to submit to authority—not as punishment, but so you can ultimately be in authority.

Paul and the Unbelieving Believers

Have you ever met an unbelieving believer? There can be two people sitting side by side on the same pew, hearing the same message, and one will believe it and the other won't. However, if you asked these two churchgoers if they are believers, both would say, "Of course!"

Yet what would happen if you followed up with a more specific question, such as, "Do you believe it's God's will to heal you?" Perhaps one would reply, "Definitely," while the other would say, "Well, if it's God's will." Both are professing believers, but one is an *unbelieving* believer.

Paul once had a bewildering experience while ministering to some disciples in Ephesus. (See Acts 19:1–7.) These people were "believers"—but *what* did they believe? It turned out that they believed in a baptism of repentance, like John the Baptist had preached. But this was incomplete knowledge at best. Sensing that something was missing in their Christian experience, Paul asked, *"Did you receive the Holy Spirit when you believed?"* (Acts 19:2). They admitted, *"We have not so much as heard whether there is a Holy Spirit"* (Acts 19:2).

There was no way these people could *believe* in or *receive* the power of the Holy Spirit, because they had never even *heard* of Him! There was no way for faith to rise in their hearts concerning the Spirit, since *"faith comes by hearing"* (Romans 10:17).

But when Paul brought them the *full* gospel, the response was immediate: *"When they heard this, they were baptized in the name of the Lord Jesus. And when Paul* had laid hands on them, the Holy Spirit came upon them, and they spoke with tongues and prophesied" (Acts 9:5–6).

These believers had first accepted and believed the message they heard about John's baptism. And when they were exposed to a more complete revelation, they believed that, as well. Not content to remain stuck on some spiritual plateau of partial revelation, they pressed on "from one degree of glory to another" (2 Corinthians 3:18 ESV).

My friend, I pray you are hungry for more of the Lord today, eager to embrace new insights from His Word. God wants to give you more and more light, so that your life shines "ever brighter" for Him: "The path of the just is like the shining sun, that shines ever brighter unto the perfect day" (Proverbs 4:18).

9

ALL THINGS ARE POSSIBLE

Unbelief hinders God's miracles and the exercise of our authority as believers. (See Mark 6:1–6.) Today, Americans tend to be skeptical concerning the Lord's supernatural power, while many believers in Third-World countries are full of faith and expectancy toward the things of God.

Jesus knew what it was like to work His miracles in the midst of a "*faithless generation*"—but miracles happened nevertheless:

Then one of the crowd answered and said, "Teacher, I brought You my son, who has a mute spirit. And wherever it seizes him, it throws him down; he foams at the mouth, gnashes his teeth, and becomes rigid. So I spoke to Your disciples, that they should cast it out, but they could not." He answered him and said, "O faithless generation, how long shall I be with you? How long shall I bear with you? Bring him to Me." Then they brought him to Him. And when he saw Him, immediately the spirit convulsed him, and he fell on the ground and wallowed, foaming at the mouth. So He asked his father, "How long has this been happening to him?" And he said, "From childhood. And often he has thrown him both into the fire and into the water to destroy him. But if You can do anything, have compassion on us and help us." Jesus said to him, "If you can believe, all things are possible to him who believes."

(Mark 9:17–23)

This man had first tried bringing his demon-possessed son to Jesus' disciples, but they were unable to cast out the demon. The disciples had successfully cast out demons on other occasions, for they later asked Jesus, *"Why could we not cast it out?"* (verse 28). Genuinely surprised at their failure, they wanted to find out what had gone wrong this time.

Jesus explained, *"This kind can come out by nothing but prayer and fasting"* (Mark 9:29). But, once again, faith was the missing ingredient, as we see in Matthew's parallel account of this same story:

Jesus said to them, "[It is] because of your unbelief; for assuredly, I say to you, if you have faith as a mustard seed, you will say to this mountain, 'Move from here to there,' and it will move; and nothing will be impossible for you."

(Matthew 17:20)

Although Jesus was happy to cast out the demon Himself, He seemed annoyed that His disciples and others in the *"faithless generation"* were unable to stand in their *own* authority to get the job done. You see, Jesus had *already given* His disciples authority to defeat demonic spirits:

*Jesus summoned His twelve disciples and **gave them authority over unclean spirits, to cast them out**, and to heal every kind of disease and every kind of sickness.*   (Matthew 10:1 NASB)

Even though the disciples had all the authority they needed, they didn't know how to *use* it. How similar this is to the experience of many Christians today!

Help My Unbelief!

While addressing this father's desperate request, Jesus makes a stunning statement about the power of faith in God: *"All things are possible to him who believes"* (Mark 9:23). In this passage, Jesus is not referring to *some* things, but He says that *"all things"* are possible when we truly believe God and activate His promises!

What is your level of faith today? Do you believe God can do *some* things but not *other* things? Or do you truly grasp the magnificent truth that He can do *all* things through your faith?

It seems that many people have faith for just about anything—except for the miracle they need the most. Perhaps they have faith for healing, but what they really need is a financial breakthrough. Or maybe they have plenty of faith for God's financial provision, yet they struggle to believe He can change their wayward children.

This father was very honest about his level of faith. With tears in his eyes, he immediately told Jesus, *"Lord, I believe; help my unbelief!"* (Mark 9:24). The man was a believer, or he wouldn't have brought his son for deliverance in the first place. Yet he recognized that although he *believed*, he needed Jesus' help with his *unbelief*.

Friend, perhaps you are feeling the very same way today. You want to believe Jesus for the miracle you need, and you *do* believe Him—up to a point. However, you're honest enough to see that your faith is mixed with doubt, and your belief is mixed with unbelief. If so, I encourage you to do what this anxious father did: Bring Jesus whatever faith you can muster, and ask Him to supply the rest!

And never forget that the Scriptures are very clear about what it takes to gain greater faith. We're told in in Romans 10:17: *"Faith comes by hearing, and hearing by the word of God."* So, if you want to grow in your faith for a healing, a financial breakthrough, or a restored relationship, you need to read, believe, and meditate on the Bible's specific promises for you in those areas.

The Greek word Paul uses for *"hearing"* in this passage is *akoē*. This word means much more than just hearing sermons or being able to quote what God says in the Bible. *Akoē* implies that we perceive, comprehend, and understand what God's Word says. And this only comes when we take time to consider and attend to His Word.

A Spirit of Blindness

Years ago, a young woman came to our church for prayer because she was going blind. I sensed that there was a demonic component to her illness and began to minister deliverance to her. She didn't really believe in deliverance, nor did she think a Christian could be oppressed by a demon. But she wanted prayer for her impending blindness, so she agreed to let me pray.

I told her I was going to rebuke the demon spirit that was causing her condition. And as I put my hand on her head and commanded that evil spirit to leave her, she suddenly jumped and gasped. The demon left, and her eyes were healed!

The young woman had no idea a demon spirit was trying to take her sight. It shocked her and scared her. But when she realized her sight had returned, she began to praise God for setting her free. She went back to her doctors and had some tests run, only to find there was no longer anything wrong with her.

This woman was a believer, but she had unbelief concerning deliverance. If the truth were known, many believers have one area or another where they don't believe what the Scriptures say about their authority in Christ. Instead of believing the *entire* good news of the gospel, they pick and choose the portions they accept. And often, the parts they've rejected are the ones they need the most.

God's Delegated Power

Authority is delegated power. As an illustration, think of yourself as a business owner. If you hire managers for your business, you are delegating authority to them to act on your behalf, as long as it's in the best interest of the business. In the same way, God has delegated to us the legal right to take ownership of His creation and do business in His name.

As individuals, we each have different circumstances. If you are raising children, God has given you His delegated authority over your family. Whether you realize it or not, you have a responsibility to take authority over anything that comes against your spouse or children. Likewise, God has given us His authority to defeat Satan's attacks on our health or our finances.

Too often, we think our authority depends on our own worthiness or strength. The devil points to our failings and inadequacies, and we back away from exercising our authority. But when this happens, we're losing sight of the fact that our authority is not dependent on our *own* righteousness or goodness but rather on the righteousness we have *in Christ*. (See 2 Corinthians 5:21.)

His Exceedingly Great Power

Just as our authority isn't dependent on our own righteousness, it isn't dependent on our own strength. Instead, it relies on the *delegated power* we've received from

God. Never forget: The effectiveness of any delegated power depends on the force standing behind it. That's good news, for our power is delegated from *God*, and it's *His* power we're relying upon.

Jesus said, *"Behold, **I give you the authority** to trample on serpents and scorpions, and **over all the power of the enemy**, and **nothing** shall by any means hurt you"* (Luke 10:19). In the mighty name of Jesus, we have *His* power and authority over every satanic scheme.

Jesus isn't just a *little bit* more powerful than the devil! He has been given *"**all** authority"* in heaven and on earth. (See Matthew 28:18.) With an unparalleled place of honor, He is seated *"**far above** all principality and power and might and dominion, and every name that is named, not only in this age but also in that which is to come"* (Ephesians 1:21). And because we are positioned in Christ, we are seated above the devil, as well. God *"raised us from the dead along with Christ and seated us with him in the heavenly realms because we are united with Christ Jesus"* (Ephesians 2:6 NLT).

We never have to feel like we're helpless victims at the hands of Satan. In fact, when we submit ourselves to God and resist the devil, he *must* flee from us. (See James 4:7.) We have the right to use Jesus' authority over every evil principality or power that opposes God's purposes for our lives.

However, we must have a *spiritual revelation* of these great truths if they are to be effective in our lives. Paul prayed that the believers in Ephesus would have the eyes of their heart opened to see *"what is the **exceeding greatness of His power toward us who believe**, according to the working of His mighty power"* (Ephesians 1:19). In *The Message* paraphrase of this passage, Paul prayed that their eyes would be *"focused and clear, so that you can see exactly what it is he is calling you to do, grasp the immensity of this glorious way of life he has for his followers, oh, the utter extravagance of his work in us who trust him—endless energy, boundless strength!"*

Take a few minutes to think about what this means. When your eyes are spiritually enlightened, you will be able to see the *"glorious way[s] of life"* God has planned for you. You will finally see *"the utter extravagance of his work"* in you, because you trust Him. And the end result will be amazing: *"endless energy, boundless strength!"*

I encourage you to meditate on this entire passage (see Ephesians 1:15–23), perhaps comparing several different versions. Pray the prayer Paul prayed, asking God to open your spiritual eyes to His awesome power and the wonderful life He has for you.

Be sure to notice that the great power described here isn't available to just anyone—it's given *"toward us who* ***believe"*** (Ephesians 1:19). If we don't *believe* we've been given God's power, it won't be activated in our life. As Jesus explained to two blind men one day, *"According to your faith let it be to you"* (Matthew 9:29).

Believe Him today!

10

A GENTILE'S REVELATION

Have you ever encountered a situation where people who'd grown up with the things of God were surprisingly dull or resistant to the faith message, while a new convert—or even someone you thought to be an unbeliever— was much more receptive? Jesus had experiences like this.

When Jesus visited His hometown of Nazareth, the people who had watched Him grow up as a young boy struggled to see Him as their Messiah and Healer. *"He marveled because of their unbelief"* (Mark 6:6); and their lack of faith caused them to miss out on the full extent of His miracle-working power: *"He could do no mighty work there, except that He laid His hands on a few sick people and healed them"* (verse 5).

But in contrast with the chilly reception Jesus received in Nazareth, we see a much different account one day when He entered the town of Capernaum: *"A centurion came to Him, pleading with Him, saying, 'Lord, my servant is lying at home paralyzed, dreadfully tormented'"* (Matthew 8:5–6).

This man was a Roman. He hadn't grown up in the Jewish synagogues, so He didn't have any knowledge of Old Testament Scripture. Yet somehow he recognized that Jesus held the key to his servant's healing.

Friend, there is not one instance in the Bible where someone came to Jesus for healing and He told them no. And in this story, Jesus told the centurion, without a moment's hesitation, "*I will come and heal him*" (Matthew 8:7). It is His will for us to walk in health!

Most people would have rejoiced in Jesus' willingness to come to the servant's sickbed and heal him, but the centurion came up with an even *better* plan: "*Lord, I am not worthy that You should come under my roof. But only speak a word, and my servant will be healed*" (Matthew 8:8).

The centurion recognized that there was no need for Jesus to come and lay hands on his servant; nor was any lengthy prayer time needed. He saw that Jesus needed only to "*speak the word*" (KJV), and the servant would be healed.

How did the centurion have such a profound insight into the nature of faith, when many of the "religious" people of Jesus' day totally missed it? It is because he understood the principle of *authority*.

> For I **also am a man under authority**, having soldiers under me. And I say to this one, "Go," and he goes; and to another, "Come," and he comes; and to my servant, "Do this," and he does it. (Matthew 8:9)

Jesus was stunned by this man's answer. Just as He had "*marveled*" at the unbelief of the people of Nazareth, He "*marveled*" at the centurion's revelation on the true nature of faith.

> When Jesus heard it, He **marveled**, and said to those who followed, "Assuredly, I say to you, **I have not found such great faith, not even in Israel!**" (Matthew 8:10)

This story has a beautiful ending. Jesus told the centurion, "'Go your way; and as **you have believed, so let it be done for you.**' And his servant was healed that same hour" (verse 13). The centurion understood the connection between authority and faith, and he quickly received the miracle He needed from the Lord.

Jesus is making this same promise to you and me today: "*As you have believed, so let it be done for you.*" So make sure you believe the truth of His Word, not the lies of the devil!

Learning from the Centurion

There is so much we can learn from this story. Sometimes people who hear about a believer's authority become utterly frustrated when they do not get results. But usually, the reason is very simple: *It is impossible to successfully walk in authority if we don't first understand and practice submission to authority.*

This was easy for the centurion to grasp. He realized he had been given a certain degree of authority from his military chain of command. But He knew it was *delegated* authority—the result of being *under* authority to his superiors and, ultimately, to the Roman emperor.

The centurion saw this same principle at work in the life of Jesus. The reason Jesus had such authority was the fact that He had willingly placed Himself under His Father's authority.

Notice that the centurion raised a very important issue when he told Jesus, *"Lord, I am not worthy that You should come under my roof"* (Matthew 8:8). The devil has convinced many Christians today that they are *unworthy* to receive anything from God. He accuses them and points out all the ways they've fallen short of God's best for them. This tactic often keeps people from drawing near to the Lord and boldly bringing Him their petitions.

But what does the Bible say about this? Does God heal people, grant financial breakthroughs, or perform other miracles based on the "merit" system? Does He weigh your "goodness" when deciding whether to answer your prayers?

Friend, you need to understand this: If you are born again, you can come to the Father on the basis of *Jesus'* righteousness, not your own. Because of your position in Christ, the Bible says you have *"become the righteousness of God in Him"* (2 Corinthians 5:21). You can't get any more "worthy" than that!

You see, it's through the blood of Jesus that you can boldly approach *"the throne of grace"* (Hebrews 4:16). You aren't called to pray in your own name or your own worthiness, but in the mighty name of *Jesus*—God's beloved Son, in whom He is well pleased. (See Matthew 3:17.)

So quit using your "unworthiness" as an excuse for not having audacious faith. When you stand in the worthiness of Jesus, you can be confident that the Father will hear and answer your prayers.

What Are You Doing?

Not only was the centurion a person of faith; he also was a person of action. He didn't just sit passively at home, hoping Jesus would pay him a visit. Instead, the centurion actively sought out Jesus and *"came to Him"* (Matthew 8:5). And he recognized that his servant wouldn't be healed unless Jesus did something: *"Speak the word"* (verse 8 KJV), he said.

It shouldn't surprise us that the centurion's faith was active rather than passive, because true faith will *always* manifest in corresponding actions: *"As the body without the spirit is dead, so faith without works is dead also"* (James 2:26).

I remember a time when Jeanne and I had been praying for a woman in the church to be healed, and Jeanne asked her one day, "What are you *doing* concerning your healing?"

Seemingly stunned by this question, the woman replied, "What do you mean, 'doing'? I believe God can heal me."

"Of course God can heal you," Jeanne persisted, "but that's not what I asked. What are doing to cooperate with Him in this?"

Sadly, the woman didn't understand. It was commendable that she believed God could heal her, but she was doing absolutely nothing to exercise her authority as a believer. While she was waiting on God to touch her body, He was waiting on her to take steps of faith and position herself for healing.

Although this woman was believing that God would manifest her healing, she ended up dying nevertheless. This really shook some people's faith. Everyone remarked about what a good person she was—a devout Christian and a sincere believer. Yes, she was all those things. She believed God for her salvation and probably for many other things, yet she didn't understand how to believe Him and act upon His promises for her healing.

Faith Comes by Hearing

So what can you do if you're a believer but discover you have an area of unbelief in your life? The key, as Romans 10:17 tells us, is to listen to the Word of God, for *"faith comes by hearing, and hearing by the word of God."* When we identify an area of unbelief in ourselves, we must commit to submerging ourselves in God's promises on that subject. This starts with looking at every Scripture we can find on the subject, and then reading that truth and listening to that truth spoken aloud. We may have to take the additional step of finding books, CDs, podcasts, or other resources to help in the process.

After I got saved, I was still in the liquor business, and the Lord told me to stay in it until He moved me away from it. As I drove my route from one liquor store and bar to another, I would listen to tapes of preaching and teaching. Every available moment, I kept feeding myself the Word of God.

We will never overcome areas of unbelief unless we saturate ourselves with what the Word says concerning that area. This may require us to read or listen to the Bible for hours at a time, but it will be well worth it. Our mind will be renewed, and our life will be transformed. (See Romans 12:2.)

Have you ever recalled a song many years after you last heard it? The song became familiar and was imprinted in your memory because you listened to it hundreds or even thousands of times. Faith comes in a similar way. As you hear the promises of God's Word and let them sink deeply into your heart, the Holy Spirit will be able to call them to your mind when you need them the most.

Enlightened by the Spirit

As important as it is to stand on God's promises in Scripture, we also need the Holy Spirit to teach us. God's Word describes the authority we have in Christ, but we still must allow the Spirit to enlighten us regarding how to exercise that authority and power.

Seeing the vital importance of this supernatural revelation, Paul told the believers in Ephesus that he was praying...

> ...that the God of our Lord Jesus Christ, the Father of glory, may give to you a spirit of wisdom and of **revelation** in the knowledge of Him. **I pray that the eyes of your heart may be enlightened**, so that you will know what is the hope of His calling, what are the riches of the glory of His inheritance in the saints, and what is **the surpassing greatness of His power toward us who believe**. (Ephesians 1:17–19 NASB)

Oh, how we need this kind of revelation in the church today! When we realize that we have power and authority over demon spirits, we become enlightened in that area, and they cannot torment us anymore. However, unless the Spirit of God enlightens us, the enemy will mercilessly torment us mentally, emotionally, and physically until we learn to stand our ground.

Many people accept the notion that they will catch a cold or the flu every year. Others worry that they will develop cancer, diabetes, or heart problems, because those diseases "run in their family." But as we become enlightened about our authority, we won't stand for this kind of thinking anymore. We will *take captive every thought to make it obedient to Christ* (2 Corinthians 10:5 NIV).

My wife, Jeanne, used to have sinus problems. As long as I have known her, she has had experienced painful sinus symptoms; and at times she was so sick she couldn't even leave the house. However, God enlightened her in this area several years ago, and she realized that she had authority over this area of her life. Ever since she stood in faith to exercise that authority, she hasn't had any further problems with her sinuses.

My friend, perhaps you're dealing with some kind of long-standing problem, as Jeanne experienced with her sinuses. Instead of an issue with your health, however, it may be a struggle with your finances, your marriage, or your children. But I want you to know today that the Holy Spirit can enlighten your spiritual eyes to the authority you've been given in that area for victory. Don't believe the devil's lie that you must accept defeat!

11

THE BASIC KEY TO VICTORY

Throughout the Bible, we see that God's people are often engaged in spiritual battles. And as believers, we, too, will face battles. This war is not something we can opt out of. No "conscientious objectors" are allowed. Whether we like it or not, or even realize what is happening, we have a fierce enemy who comes *"to steal, and to kill, and to destroy"* (John 10:10).

When we're under attack, it's not a time to be timid. We've been given powerful spiritual weapons that are *"mighty in God for pulling down strongholds"* (2 Corinthians 10:4). And the Bible describes amazing armor that is designed to protect us from head to toe against Satan's onslaughts. (See Ephesians 6:10–18.)

Countless Bible verses promise us *victory* when we follow God's plan. Here are just a few examples:

+ *"You are of God, little children, and have overcome them, because He who is in you is greater than he who is in the world."* (1 John 4:4)

+ *"Whatever is born of God overcomes the world. And this is the victory that has overcome the world—our faith."* (1 John 5:4)

+ *"If God is for us, who can be against us?...In all these things we are more than conquerors through Him who loved us."* (Romans 8:31, 37)

◆ *"Thanks be to God who always leads us in triumph in Christ."* (2 Corinthians 2:14)

Although God assures us of victory, it will not always be automatic or easy. Faith and obedience will be required, and we must be *bold* in confronting the enemy, as Jesus warned: *"From the days of John the Baptist until now the kingdom of heaven suffers violence, and the violent take it by force"* (Matthew 11:12).

The Simple Formula

Much could be written about the subject of spiritual warfare, but most of it can be boiled down to a simple, but profound, formula: *"Submit to God. Resist the devil and he will flee from you"* (James 4:7). Notice that this is all about a believer's authority in Christ. When we submit ourselves to God, we have authority to resist and rebuke the enemy. The Scriptures are full of examples of this principle.

In Exodus 17:8–13, we find that Joshua and the Israelites were victorious in their battle against the Amalekites because Moses stood on the top of the hill with *"the rod of God"* (Exodus 17:9) in his hand. The rod signified that the Israelites were submitted to God's authority and dependent on Him for victory.

In Joshua 5:13–15, Joshua was confronted with a mighty warrior angel with his sword drawn, ready for battle. Stunned by the sight of this powerful creature, Joshua asked, *"Are You for us or for our adversaries?"* (verse 13). The angel replied, *"No, but as Commander of the army of the LORD I have now come"* (verse 14).

There's a great lesson here: The real question isn't whether God is *"for us"*, but whether we are fully submitted to Him. Joshua responded correctly, ready to submit and obey: *"Joshua fell on his face to the earth and worshiped, and said to Him, 'What does my Lord say to His servant?'"* (Joshua 5:14).

In Joshua chapter 7, the Israelites faced an embarrassing defeat at the hands of the small town of Ai. How could this be? In the previous chapter, they had won a great victory over the larger city of Jericho; so defeating Ai should have been easy in comparison.

When Joshua cried out for an explanation concerning this defeat, God informed him about sin in the camp:

> *Israel has sinned, and they have also transgressed My covenant which I commanded them. For they have even taken some of the accursed things, and have both stolen and deceived; and they have also put it among their own stuff. Therefore*

the children of Israel could not stand before their enemies, but turned their backs before their enemies, because they have become doomed to destruction. Neither will I be with you anymore, unless you destroy the accursed from among you. Get up, sanctify the people, and say, "Sanctify yourselves for tomorrow, because thus says the LORD God of Israel: 'There is an accursed thing in your midst, O Israel; you cannot stand before your enemies until you take away the accursed thing from among you.'" (Joshua 7:11–13)

What a vital lesson about a believer's authority! Because the Israelites allowed sin in the camp, they were not able to stand before their enemies. In failing to fully submit themselves to God, they had no authority for victory in battle.

Conditions to God's Promises

Over the years, I've often had people come to me and say that they had claimed one of God's promises in the Bible, but it just didn't come to pass. Since the Lord is always faithful to His Word, I knew that something must be amiss in their application.

What people often fail to see is that God's promises nearly always have conditions attached. He says, in essence, "If you do *this*, I'll do *that*." And if we try to claim a promise without first doing our part, there's no way we're going to get what we've asked for.

For example, look at Jesus' great promise in Mark 11:22–23:

Have faith in God. For assuredly, I say to you, whoever says to this mountain, "Be removed and be cast into the sea," and does not doubt in his heart, but believes that those things he says will be done, he will have whatever he says.

First, this verse says you must speak to the mountain that's in your way, telling it to be removed. This doesn't mean grumbling about the mountain, telling your pastor about the mountain, or notifying the church prayer chain about the mountain. You must *personally* speak to your mountain in faith if you're to claim the promise in this verse.

Next, Jesus says you must truly *believe*, without doubting in your heart. Without faith, our act of speaking to the mountain would just be a matter of superstition or a hocus-pocus kind of formula. Only when we believe, with authentic faith, can we be assured that we will have whatever we say.

So how do we know our faith is genuine and we've met this condition of believing in our heart? Jesus continues explaining this in the next verse:

> *Therefore I say to you, whatever things you ask when you pray, believe that you receive them, and you will have them.* (Mark 11:24)

The *New Living Translation* makes the Greek verb tense clearer here: "I tell you, you can pray for anything, and if you **believe that you've received it**, it will be yours." Other translations verify Jesus' message here that true faith is not just believing that you *will* receive something but believing that you *"have received"* (NASB, NIV, ESV) what you're asking for.

Do you see how crucial this distinction is? Many Christians think they are praying in *faith*, when they're actually just praying in *hope*. Hope is a wonderful thing, but it has to do with something in the future. Faith, if it is genuine, connects us to God's promises right *now*! (See Hebrews 11:1.)

More than Lip Service

If you've spent much time hanging out with longtime Christians, you've probably already discovered a troubling fact: Often, the *reality* of our lives doesn't match our *rhetoric*. For example, it's pretty easy to sing "I Surrender All" in worship services; but too often, that testimony isn't demonstrated in our lives.

When we give lip service to God's truth without really believing it in our hearts, we're sure to be disappointed with the results. And sometimes we've picked up a useful formula from a true man or woman of God—but the formula hasn't become a part of our own life.

Look what happened to some men who tried to use the name of Jesus to cast out demons, just because they saw it work for Paul:

> *Then some of the itinerant Jewish exorcists took it upon themselves to call the name of the Lord Jesus over those who had evil spirits, saying, "We exorcise you by the Jesus whom Paul preaches." Also there were seven sons of Sceva, a Jewish chief priest, who did so. And the evil spirit answered and said, "Jesus I know, and Paul I know; but who are you?" Then the man in whom the evil spirit was leaped*

on them, overpowered them, and prevailed against them, so that they fled out of
that house naked and wounded.   (Acts 19:13–16)

Friend, the name of Jesus is incredibly powerful, as we will explore in a later chapter. But our authority to use Jesus' name is dependent on submitting to Him and walking in an intimate covenant relationship with Him. When you do this, you can confidently *"resist the devil and he will flee from you"* (James 4:7). Or, as this is paraphrased in *The Message,* you can *"yell a loud **no** to the Devil and watch him scamper"*!

12

QUALIFICATIONS FOR USING YOUR AUTHORITY

When Jesus told Peter, "*On this rock I will build My church*" (Matthew 16:18), He wasn't calling Peter a rock. Instead, the rock Jesus referred to was the revelation of who He was. That's why Paul wrote, "*No other foundation can anyone lay than that which is laid, which is Jesus Christ*" (1 Corinthians 3:11). And Jesus also is the precious "*chief cornerstone*" (1 Peter 2:6) that we as "*living stones*" (1 Peter 2:5) must relate to in God's house.

Although this revelation of Jesus is very basic and fundamental, many professing Christians have missed it. To them, Jesus is merely an historical character or a figure from a Sunday school lesson. However, the true church must be built upon a revelation of the true Jesus. He is the King of Kings and the Lord of Lords. (See Revelation 17:14; 19:16.) He is the Lion of the tribe of Judah (see Revelation 5:5) and the holy Son of God, our Savior (see Luke 2:11).

The gates of hell will never prevail against a church—or an individual believer—built upon this kind of authentic revelation of who Jesus is. There's no way to use "*the keys of the kingdom of heaven*" (Matthew 16:19) unless we have a deep personal relationship with Jesus. This is the first qualification for exercising authority on Jesus' behalf—knowing who He is and what He has done for us.

Notice that Jesus didn't say He was giving us only *one* key to His kingdom. He said there are multiple keys, which unlock numerous doors. Many Christians are thrilled just to get the key that opens the doorway to heaven when they die, but Jesus has much more in mind for us. Long before we get to heaven, He wants us to unlock His kingdom's prosperity, health, and other blessings.

Jesus told His disciples, *"It is your Father's good pleasure to give you the kingdom"* (Luke 12:32). He didn't mean just *some* of the kingdom—He meant the *whole* kingdom! But in order to unlock all of God's kingdom blessings, you need *all* of the keys, and you must believe *all* of His promises.

True faith says, "I've read or heard God's promise. I believe it. I am going to act upon it and then declare the victory!" However, many people are still waiting to *see* something or *feel* something before they believe God or take a step of faith. Head knowledge or intellectual assent to the truth of God's Word does not qualify as real faith.

While the first qualification for exercising authority is to have a revelation of Jesus' authority, the second qualification is that we *act upon* the authority He has given to us. We have "potential" authority at the moment of our initial salvation, but it is something that must be *activated*. In many ways, our faith and our authority are like muscles in the body—they grow stronger through use.

God has made us joint heirs with Jesus, and He expects us to act like it. As children of the Most High God, we must take our place with Jesus, far above all principalities and powers. (See Ephesians 1:21.)

Can We Rebuke the Devil?

Years ago when my family and I traveled around the country ministering and singing, I spoke on the authority of a believer in a church in Virginia. After the service, the pastor called me into his office while my wife and son waited in the van, ready to leave. He reprimanded me for teaching his people that they had authority to bind and loose the forces of Satan.

To support his view, the pastor used the story of the archangel Michael contending with Satan over the body of Moses. (See Jude 1:9.) Jude says Michael *"dared not bring against him a reviling accusation, but said, 'The Lord rebuke you!'"* The pastor tried to convince me that this example showed the proper way to use God's authority in resisting the devil. He had taught his congregation that they should never rebuke the devil directly. Instead, they should ask God to rebuke the enemy *for* them. In essence, the pastor was saying that believers have no authority at all but simply must call upon God to exercise *His* authority over our troublesome circumstances.

I asked the Lord about this, because the pastor's view didn't seem to reconcile with Jesus' words to Peter in Matthew 16:19: *"I will give you the keys of the kingdom of heaven, and whatever you bind on earth will be bound in heaven, and whatever you loose on earth will be loosed in heaven."*

As I thought of this verse again, God asked me, "Who was given this promise in Matthew 16:19?"

"It was given to believers, like me," I replied.

"That's right!" the Lord assured me. "The promise here wasn't given to Michael. He is an archangel, and he does whatever he is assigned to do. But he is not created in My image and likeness; so the same promises don't apply to him. You can be confident of your authority to bind and loose, because the promise in Matthew 16:19 was written to you and not to angels."

That settled it for me, and it has been working ever since. Instead of using Michael or other angels as our model, we must realize that we're sons and daughters of God, with all the authority Jesus has promised us. The same principle is shown in Psalm 8:3–5:

> *When I consider Your heavens, the work of Your fingers, the moon and the stars, which You have ordained, what is man that You are mindful of him, and the son of man that You visit him? For You have made him a little lower than the angels, and You have crowned him with glory and honor.*

Faith in Specific Areas

Some believers have a special anointing to pray the prayer of faith for people to be healed. Others have a high degree of faith for seeing financial breakthroughs, family reconciliation, or deliverance.

When my wife, Jeanne, and I started in the ministry, it was very apparent that we each had exceptional faith for different things. She had more faith in believing God in the area of finances than I did. But I had more faith in the area of healing than she did.

Jeanne was raised in a denomination that taught that God was going to hold every sin that you ever committed against you; and, as a result, bad things could happen if God punished you or decided to teach you a lesson. So, when I first began to study the Word, Jeanne would ask me to explain the chastisement of the Lord. The more I examined this, the more I realized she had been raised with some unbalanced perspectives on God's reproofs and reprimands. In contrast, it was much easier for me to have faith concerning God's lovingkindness and His desire for us to prosper and to be in health.

When I was in high school, I wanted to be an FBI agent. I studied all of the applicant requirements, and one of them shocked me. They wanted applicants who had never fired a gun. I thought that was strange, since one of the reasons I wanted to be an FBI agent was so I could carry a weapon. When I asked about it, I was told that those who had already used firearms were more likely to have developed bad shooting habits. It's easier to teach someone to shoot correctly from the beginning than to break bad habits. The same principle applies in spiritual matters. We can learn bad habits, picking up wrong doctrines and beliefs.

When Jeanne and I first got married, I had a lot of bad habits in the area of finances. Jeanne was a giver from the start. She *loved* to give and was meticulous about giving the Lord ten cents out of every dollar. I remember the first time the Lord supernaturally met our needs. Totally out of the blue, He sent someone to our door to give us fifty dollars, and the first thing Jeanne wanted to do with it was to tithe.

I said, "Wait, Jeanne, we really do need the money, and we've only had this for a few minutes!" She found it easy to have faith in that area, but it was something I struggled with at first. I simply wasn't taught that way.

When we were building our church building, Jeanne was the one who would pay the contractors. She would tell them to come back each week, and we would pay them a certain amount.

We didn't have any money at the time, so I would ask her, "Why did you tell them that? We don't have anything to give them."

She would simply say, "We are going to pay." Finally, I decided to quit worrying and just let her handle it. It was no problem for her to act in faith, so I got out of the way and let her!

Jeanne and I learned an important lesson along the way. We saw that if someone has an area of weakness in their belief system, they may need to stand on the faith of another, such as a spouse, a prayer partner, or a friend who is stronger in that area.

By exposing ourselves to their revelation of God's Word, we can correct a weak or faulty belief system. If you know someone who has more faith in a given area than you do, call upon them to support you and bring you to a new level of faith and authority.

Growing Your Faith

The meaning of the word "believe" is frequently watered down today, even among longtime Christians. Many people say, "I believe so," when they're actually full of unbelief and double-mindedness. Those who *truly* believe will live in accordance with whatever God has said. Genuine faith understands that God's promises don't require us to *beg* Him to do something for us. On the contrary, His promises *belong to us* as believers.

Although true faith will begin as a *fact*, it always ends with an *act*. For faith to come alive, we must act on what we believe and step out in obedience to God's Word and the leading of His Spirit. This is not playacting, nor is it an attempt to convince others we have authority. When we meet God's qualifications, know His Word, and have a receptive heart and attitude, we can boldly exercise our authority and further His kingdom.

However, unbelief will keep us from accepting and using the authority God wants us to use. If we foster unbelief in our heart, we undercut and disqualify our authority. That's why we must go on the offensive and use words of faith to push unbelief out of our life. We do this by finding out what the Word says about the situation we're going through and then standing on the Word to gain victory.

As we learn to trust and obey the Lord in every situation, we will increasingly develop more confidence and more faith. Like a muscle that gets stronger through exertion, our faith will grow and our circumstances transform as we stand on the Word. Then, all of a sudden, our faith will take a quantum leap into a realm of victory we've never experienced before. Instead of a humdrum, powerless Christian life, we will lead a life of adventure; we will *"be strong, and carry out great exploits"* (Daniel 11:32).

13

YOUR AUTHORITY IN
JESUS' NAME

Nothing in this world is more powerful than the name of Jesus. Why? Because it's the key, or the "password," to our authority as believers.

The Bible says we've already been given *"every spiritual blessing in the heavenly places in Christ"* (Ephesians 1:3). Think of it: *every* spiritual blessing already belongs to us. But how do we *access* these blessings and apply them to our lives? Through faith in the name of Jesus!

In Jesus' name, we have authority over any virus, cancer, or other disease that attacks our body. We can say, "Stop, in the name of Jesus! You'll go no further." The enemy has to obey when we stand in the authority and power of Jesus' name.

Paul tells us *"that at the name of Jesus every knee will bow...every tongue will confess that Jesus Christ is Lord, to the glory of God the Father"* (Philippians 2:10–11 NASB). Every demon will have to bow before His name. Every problem will have to bow. Every financial need will have to bow. Every divisive spirit will have to bow. *Everything*!

The power and authority delegated to you in Jesus' name does not make you immune to the enemy's attacks. However, it does give you the ability to overcome them. John wrote, *"He who is in you is greater than he who is in the world"* (1 John 4:4). You can live in victory in the name of Jesus!

No wonder the devil *hates* to hear that name. No wonder he does everything he can to discredit it, ridicule it, and water it down. As a result, some believers have lost their boldness to use the name of Jesus. They don't mind speaking to their unsaved friends about "God" or their "higher power," but they are intimidated from declaring their confidence in the name of Jesus.

The Early Church

The first-century Christians didn't have the advantages of modern technology to spread the gospel. They had no TV, radio, Internet, cell phones, or iPads. There were no airplanes to take them from country to country.

Despite lacking our modern conveniences, the early church turned the world upside down for Jesus. (See Acts 17:5–7.) In just a few centuries, they had spread the gospel to the known world. From Jesus' original handful of followers, the community of faith had grown to millions.

What was the secret of the early Christians? I'm sure a number of things could be cited as reasons for their success; but one stands out above them all: *They understood the power they had in the name of Jesus!* Look at these amazing examples:

- On the day of Pentecost, Peter preached, *"Whoever calls on the **name of the** **Lord** shall be saved"* (Acts 2:21). In its simplest terms, the gospel is summed up by individuals who call on the name of Jesus to be saved.

- Peter told the new converts to repent and *"be baptized in the **name of Jesus Christ** for the remission of sins"* (Acts 2:38). From the first moment of their salvation, these believers were transferred into God's kingdom by Jesus' name.

- The lame man sitting outside the temple was told, *"In the **name of Jesus Christ** of Nazareth, rise up and walk"* (Acts 3:6). He was healed through the power of faith in Jesus' name. Peter explained to the crowd, *"**His name**, through faith in **His name**, has made this man strong, whom you see and know"* (Acts 3:16, 4:10).

- Peter preached that there is only salvation in the name of Jesus: *"Nor is there salvation in any other, for there is **no other name** under heaven given among men by which we must be saved"* (Acts 4:12).

+ The religious leaders summoned the apostles "*and commanded them not to speak at all nor teach in the **name of Jesus**" (Acts 4:18). The name of Jesus was a threat to religious establishment!

+ The followers of Christ asked God to give them boldness to preach the Word, "*by stretching out Your hand to heal, and that signs and wonders may be done through the **name of Your holy Servant Jesus**" (Acts 4:30). We would see a lot more signs and wonders in the church today if we understood the power in the name of Jesus.

+ When the leaders of the Sanhedrin "*had called for the apostles and beaten them, they commanded that they should not speak in the **name of Jesus**, and let them go. So they departed from the presence of the council, rejoicing that they were **counted worthy to suffer shame for His name**. And daily in the temple, and in every house, they did not cease teaching and **preaching Jesus** as the Christ*" (Acts 5:40–42). The name of Jesus not only brings salvation and miracles—it also results in *persecution*. (See, for example, Acts 9:15–16.)

+ In Samaria, people "*believed Philip as he preached the things concerning the kingdom of God and **the name of Jesus Christ**" (Acts 8:12). The good news of the kingdom focuses on the power and authority available in Jesus' name.

+ Barnabas and Paul are described as "*men who have risked their lives for the **name of our Lord Jesus Christ**" (Acts 15:26). Using Jesus' name is not just a badge of authority; it's also a commitment to lay down our lives for Him.

+ After being followed for many days by a demonized slave girl, Paul finally turned to her and said directly to the evil spirit, "*I command you in the **name of Jesus Christ** to come out of her*" (Acts 16:18). But, as we saw earlier, things didn't turn out well for some Jewish exorcists who tried to use Jesus' name without truly submitting to Him. (See Acts 19:13–17.)

This is quite a list, isn't it? Salvation, baptism, healing, deliverance, prayer—the church in Acts did all these things, and much more, in Jesus' name.

Reclaiming the Power of His Name

Despite the overwhelming evidence of how the early church unleashed God's miracle-working power through the name of Jesus, we've somehow drifted far from this practice today. Yes, we put "in the name of Jesus" at the end of our prayers, but do we truly believe in the power of that name?

Take a look at what the Bible says about the name of Jesus:

1. Jesus' name was prophesied and confirmed by God Himself.

Two verses in Isaiah specifically mention the "name" of the coming Messiah:

*Therefore the Lord Himself will give you a sign: behold, the virgin shall conceive and bear a Son, and shall call His **name** Immanuel.* (Isaiah 7:14)

Matthew quotes this Old Testament prophecy in relationship to Jesus, and he mentions that the meaning of Immanuel is *"God with us"* (Matthew 1:23).

Unto us a Child is born, unto us a Son is given; and the government will be upon His shoulder. And His name will be called Wonderful, Counselor, Mighty God, Everlasting Father, Prince of Peace. (Isaiah 9:6)

Before Jesus was born, an angel of the Lord told Joseph what to name Him: *"She will bring forth a Son, and you shall call His **name** JESUS, for He will save His people from their sins"* (Matthew 1:21).

If we are going to use Jesus' name with authority, we have to know what His name means and why it is important to us. Does the name of Jesus really mean anything to you? It should! If it doesn't mean anything to you, it certainly won't mean anything to a demon, to sickness, to relationship conflict, or to financial lack.

In the book of Acts, we see that demons recognized the power and authority of the name of Jesus when people spoke it in authority. However, the name of Jesus had no impact when spoken by people who didn't really know Him, who didn't grasp what His name meant.

What a lesson! The name of Jesus can't be used as a mere formula or "magic" word. It needs to be esteemed as sacred, holy, and precious to you if it is going to have any impact on your problems or on the world.

When I was a little boy, I learned the power and authority of my father's name. He was very well respected in the community, and I could go to stores and get anything just by using his name. Whatever I wanted, all I had to do was sign for it. You see, my father's name stood for something, and I was blessed by the right to use that name because of my relationship with him.

I also could use my father's name because I gladly identified myself as his son. That's the key to being able to use Jesus' name, as well. When we understand our position in Christ, we will have boldness to use His name with authority.

Some years ago, I met a lady whose last name was Hurst. She was a member of the famed William Randolph Hurst family, heirs of the newspaper fortune. In the 1950s, William Randolph Hurst heard Billy Graham preach, and he was impressed. He called his editors and said to "puff" Graham, which meant to build up Graham and promote his reputation in the newspapers. God used William Randolph Hurst and all his syndicated newspapers to promote Billy Graham and make him a household name around the country, and eventually around the world. The name "Graham" ended up standing for something, impacting countless millions of people over many decades.

I live in Arkansas, where the Wal-Mart and Sam's Club chains are based. The name of Sam Walton came to stand for something, first in Arkansas, and now all over the world. In a similar way, names like Jacuzzi, Nike, or Apple all stand for something. These names are important because the companies have achieved success and recognition.

But there is no name that comes close to the success and recognition of the name of Jesus. His name and fame fill the entire universe. And one day every knee will bow down at His name and declare that He is Lord. (See Philippians 2:10–11.)

2. Jesus' name means "God with us" and "God in us."

Believers need to recognize the powerful fact that God is *with us* in every situation. That's what the name Immanuel means. (See Isaiah 7:14; Matthew 1:23.)

But Jesus also is the *Christ*, which means "the Anointed One" or "Messiah." "Christ" is Jesus' title, not His last name. This has a powerful significance for us as believers. We are called to be "Christians," or little anointed ones! Although the name was originally used in derision (see Acts 11:26), we can now call ourselves "Christians" as a badge of honor, identifying with our Lord, Christ Jesus.

It is vital to realize that, in addition to God being *with* us, He now lives in us through the Holy Spirit. That's why Paul wrote, *"It is no longer I who live, but Christ lives in me"* (Galatians 2:20). And he encouraged the Christians in Colossae with the same truth, *"Christ in you, the hope of glory"* (Colossians 1:27).

Do you see how powerful this truth is? You are not alone as you try to live the Christian life. In fact, it's not about *trying* at all—it's about *trusting*. Christ lives in you, and He is fully capable of producing love, joy, peace, patience, and His other attributes in your life today. (See Galatians 5:22–23.)

3. Jesus' name is more excellent than any other name.

We're told in Hebrews 1:1–4:

> *God, who at various times and in various ways spoke in time past to the fathers by the prophets, has in these last days spoken to us by His Son, whom He has appointed heir of all things, through whom also He made the worlds; who being the brightness of His glory and the express image of His person, and upholding all things by the word of His power, when He had by Himself purged our sins, sat down at the right hand of the Majesty on high, having become so much better than the angels, as He has by inheritance obtained a more excellent name than they.*

Jesus' name is higher and more glorious than any other name in heaven or on earth. His name is above the archangels of heaven or Satan and any principalities from hell. The name of Jesus is *"more excellent"* than any problem in your life or stronghold of the enemy.

You see, *everything* that has ever been given a name is subject to the name of Jesus. The doctors may tell you that they found a tumor. But "tumor" is a name, and so it is subject to the name of Jesus. Cancer, fever, diabetes, fear, poverty, and conflict are all names subject to the name of Jesus.

Ephesians 1:22–23 says it so well: "[God] *put **all** things under His feet, and gave Him to be head over **all** things to the church, which is His body, the fullness of Him who fills all in all."* All things, not just some things, have been put under Jesus' feet. And you and I are part of His body, called to reign with Him for all eternity!

4. Jesus' name is the key to salvation and to authority over the powers of darkness.

Have you ever wondered why Satan tries so hard to discredit the name of Jesus? It's because Jesus' name is the key to our victory over him.

The disciples were amazed when they discovered this truth. Coming back from one of their first ministry trips, they exclaimed, *"Lord, even the demons are subject to us **in Your name**"* (Luke 10:17). Remember: Demons aren't subject to you because of your name, but because of His name. Satan hates the name of Jesus. He works to get people to curse and take that name in vain. And he also portrays believers as narrow-minded and bigoted if they say Jesus is the only way to salvation. (See John 14:6; Acts 4:12.)

If you simply talk to people about "religion," most of them will be agreeable when you say you believe in God. In fact, they are likely to tell you that they believe in God, too. However, many people get argumentative when you start defining who God is and then go on to say that Jesus is the only way to a relationship with God the Father.

This is not just a matter of human resistance to the gospel. Paul told us,

Even if our gospel is veiled, it is veiled to those who are perishing, whose minds the god of this age has blinded, who do not believe, lest the light of the gospel of the glory of Christ, who is the image of God, should shine on them.
(2 Corinthians 4:3–4)

Satan, *"the god of this age,"* has blinded the eyes of people *"who do not believe."* No wonder he is so intent on discrediting the name of Jesus, which is the only weapon that can defeat him and set people free.

We should expect miracles and breakthroughs through Jesus' name.

If the name of Jesus is the key to our authority, then we must learn how to use His name for the miracles and breakthroughs we need. He has delegated His authority to us as believers, and we should be filled with great expectancy:

Most assuredly, I say to you, he who believes in Me, the works that I do he will do also; and greater works than these he will do, because I go to My Father.
(John 14:12)

Through Jesus' name, we've been given the privilege to do the same miraculous works He did. Stop for a minute and consider what an awe-inspiring statement that is. And notice that Jesus also says His remarkable power will be released in our lives as we learn to pray in His name:

*Whatever you **ask in My name**, that I will do, that the Father may be glorified in the Son.*
(John 14:13)

It's only fitting that we're told to make our prayer requests in the name of Jesus, since *everything* in our lives should be done in His name: "**Whatever you do in word or deed, do all in the name of the Lord Jesus, giving thanks to God the Father through Him**" (Colossians 3:17). Other verses describe the many different ways that Jesus' name can impact our lives:

+ "*In the name of the Lord Jesus and by the Spirit of our God*" (1 Corinthians 6:11), we've been washed, sanctified, and justified.

+ "*The name of our Lord Jesus Christ*" (2 Thessalonians 1:12) is supposed to be glorified in us, and we are supposed to be glorified in Him.

+ Everyone "*who names the name of Christ*" should "*depart from iniquity*" (2 Timothy 2:19).

+ When you minister to people in need, God sees your "*labor of love which you have shown toward His name*" (Hebrews 6:10).

+ Those who are sick are told to "*call for the elders of the church, and let them pray over him, anointing him with oil in the name of the Lord*" (James 5:14).

+ Persecution is connected with Jesus' name: "*If you are reproached for the name of Christ, blessed are you, for the Spirit of glory and of God rests upon you. On their part He is blasphemed, but on your part He is glorified*" (1 Peter 4:14).

+ Those "*who believe in the name of the Son of God*" (1 John 5:13) can *know* that they have eternal life.

+ At Jesus' return, "*He* [will have] *on His robe and on His thigh a name written:* KING OF KINGS AND LORD OF LORDS" (Revelation 19:16).

+ In the New Jerusalem, Jesus' followers "*shall see His face, and His name shall be on their foreheads*" (Revelation 22:4).

My friend, we have been given authority to use the mighty name of Jesus in our daily lives. Our position in Christ is far above every satanic scheme or earthly problem. Even if circumstances look grim, messy, or even hopeless today, they are destined to line up with your position in Christ. You can use His name to find victory and overcome your circumstances.

14

THE AUTHORITY OF GOD'S WORD

J ust as we have authority in the name of Jesus, we also have authority when we stand on God's Word. Satan doesn't tremble when we share our opinions and theories. Nor does he flee just because we can quote some sermon by our pastor or a TV preacher.

But the devil does get scared when he sees that we're grounded in the truth of Scripture and able to demolish his lies. The truth will set us free from Satan's snares (see John 8:32), and the truth is found in God's Word.

Do you or a loved one need healing or deliverance today? The Bible says, "[God] *sent His word and healed them, and delivered them from their destructions*" (Psalm 107:20). We're told to give attention to God's words, because "*they are life to those who find them, and health to all their flesh*" (Proverbs 4:22). Friend, Dr. Jesus has a prescription for *you*, and it's found in His Word.

Are you facing troubling circumstances in your life? One word from Jesus can calm your raging storm. (See Mark 4:35–41.) The disciples were so terrified about their circumstances that they said to Jesus, "*Teacher, do You not care that we are perishing?*" (Mark 4:38). But after the Lord spoke peace to their circumstances, "*the wind ceased and there was a great calm*" (Mark 4:39). At this point, Jesus scolded His disciples for not exercising their own faith to calm the storm: *"Why are you so fearful? How is it that you have no faith?"* (Mark 4:40).

God has given you His Word to speak to your troublesome situations today. Whether you need a healing, a financial breakthrough, the salvation of a loved one, or some other prayer answered, remember this: *You've been given authority to speak God's Word to the "mountain" you face!*

When God speaks, *miracles happen,* as David describes so graphically in Psalm 29:3–9:

> *The God of glory thunders; the* Lord *is over many waters. The voice of the* Lord *is powerful; the voice of the* Lord *is full of majesty. The voice of the* Lord *breaks the cedars, yes, the* Lord *splinters the cedars of Lebanon. He makes them also skip like a calf, Lebanon and Sirion like a young wild ox. The voice of the* Lord *divides the flames of fire. The voice of the* Lord *shakes the wilderness; the* Lord *shakes the Wilderness of Kadesh. The voice of the* Lord *makes the deer give birth, and strips the forests bare; and in His temple everyone says, "Glory!"*

My friend, your circumstances will be transformed when you read God's Word, hear His voice, and then speak His promises!

The Word Brings Victory

In the context of describing the wonderful armor God has given us to ward off the devil's attacks (see Ephesians 6:10–17), Paul described God's Word as *"the sword of the Spirit"* (Ephesians 6:17). While the helmet, shield, and other pieces of armor are basically defensive in nature, the sword is the only *offensive* weapon described in this passage.

We see Jesus using the Word as a sword in His encounter with Satan in the wilderness at the start of His ministry. He used this sword to counteract each of the devil's three attacks: *"It is written…"* was His reply each time. (See Luke 4:1–13.)

Notice that Jesus didn't have to do a lot of scriptural research in order to discern and defeat Satan's lies. He already knew the Word, and was ready to go to battle! Can the same be said about you, my friend? Do you know God's Word well enough to counteract the enemy's lies? Can the Holy Spirit work through you to wield this mighty weapon as a *"sword"* to destroy Satan's strongholds?

I encourage you to commit yourself to taking time each day to study and meditate on God's promises in the Bible. There's no other way to stand in God's authority and be successful in spiritual warfare.

Exposing Satan's Lies

In order to understand how the Word of God enables us to defeat Satan's attacks, we need to recognize that *lying* is his most effective strategy against us. In fact, lying is not just what Satan *does*, but it's a fundamental part of who he *is*:

> *He has always hated the truth, because there is no truth in him. When he lies, it is consistent with his character; for he is a liar and the father of lies.*
>
> (John 8:44 NLT)

So, in order to defeat the devil at his game, you must know the truth well enough that you are able to recognize his deceptions. I once heard about a man who inspected money for the Federal Reserve to detect counterfeit bills. Instead of spending a lot of time learning about the various counterfeits, he said his main strategy was to know the genuine bills so well that the counterfeits would appear obvious. That should be the same approach we use in detecting the devil's lies.

Knowing this truth, how should you respond to an attack by Satan on your health? The Bible is full of promises concerning your right to healing and health as a believer, and it encourages you to *"let God be found true, though every man be found a liar"* (Romans 3:4 NASB)! That means that we need to believe the promises of the Lord instead of Satan's "lying symptoms."

Here are just a few of the Lord's great promises for your healing:

+ *"**I will restore health to you** and heal you of your wounds."* (Jeremiah 30:17)
+ *"Bless the LORD , O my soul, and forget not all His benefits…who **heals all your diseases**; who redeems your life from destruction."* (Psalm 103:2–4)
+ *"He was wounded for our transgressions, He was bruised for our iniquities; the chastisement for our peace was upon Him, and by His stripes **we are healed**."* (Isaiah 53:5)

- "[He] *Himself bore our sins in His own body on the tree, that we, having died to sins, might live for righteousness; by whose stripes* **you were healed.**" (1 Peter 2:24)

- "*Beloved, I pray that you may prosper in all things and* **be in health,** *just as your soul prospers.*" (3 John 1:2)

If you are struggling with some kind of physical sickness today, I encourage you to meditate on these verses and speak them to the circumstances in your life.

And remember: God's Word has an answer, not just for your healing, but for every problem you will ever face. It's a powerful offensive weapon that you can use to gain *victory!* Whenever you face a battle, you can find a scriptural promise to stand on, giving you authority over the enemy.

Speak the Word

We can be confident that God's Word will accomplish its intended purpose in our lives and our circumstances. The Lord tells us in Isaiah 55:11:

So shall My word be that goes forth from My mouth; it shall not return to Me void, but it shall accomplish what I please, and it shall prosper in the thing for which I sent it.

But in order to have its maximum impact, Scripture must be *believed* and *spoken.* Instead of merely treasuring the Word in our *heart* (see Psalm 119:11), we should be confessing it from our *mouth,* as Paul encourages us: "'*The word is near you, in your mouth and in your heart*' (that is, the word of faith which we preach)" (Romans 10:8). God not only has given us His written Word to *believe,* but He has also authorized us to *speak* it. Just as the centurion said to Jesus in Luke 7:7, "*Say the word, and my servant will be healed,*" you and I have been given the authority to boldly speak God's Word!

So what do you need from Jesus today? A healing? A financial miracle? A restored relationship? Deliverance from an addiction? First let Him speak His Word to you; then *you* must speak His Word to your circumstances! The miracle will come.

Remember: The God you serve is the same One who spoke the worlds into existence and said, "*Let there be light*" (Genesis 1:3; see also Hebrews 11:3). One word from Him can easily give us whatever breakthrough we need. His word is near you, in your mouth and in your heart...so speak that word!

15

YOUR AUTHORITY IN PRAYER

Without faith, it's impossible to please God (see Hebrews 11:6); and faith is also an indispensable part of standing in our authority to overcome the attacks of the enemy. First John 5:4 says, "*Whatever is born of God overcomes the world. And this is the victory that has overcome the world; our faith.*" Faith is a powerful weapon in our spiritual arsenal, and it is largely fortified through the Word of God and prayer.

Remember: Faith is a *fact*, but faith is also an *act*. Without works, faith is dead. (See James 2:26.) Faith is the title deed to your inheritance, and it means speaking to things that are not as if they are. (See Romans 4:17 KJV.)

You've been given a tremendous inheritance, but you have to recognize it and claim it. If someone dies and has given you a bequest in their will, you will probably receive a call or letter from the attorney handling the estate. They'll inform you that you've been left a bequest of some kind—a house, a piece of property, some money, or some personal items. It's something you've inherited. You have a legal right to it. It's yours now.

However, the attorney will also probably inform you that you need to *act* upon your inheritance. You may need to go to the attorney's office or the courthouse, and there will undoubtedly be papers for you to sign. The inheritance belongs to you, but you still need to claim what is yours.

The same is true with God's promises and the authority He has delegated to you. When Jesus died, he passed along this authority to you and me. It belongs to us now, but we need to step out in faith and obedience to receive our inheritance.

Power Through Prayer

If we truly believe God's promises, we will want to implement them through prayer. Even Jesus Himself—though He was the Son of God—recognized His need for regular times of prayer to the Father. Look at this stunning evidence:

+ **Early morning prayer.** *"Now in the morning, having risen a long while before daylight, He went out and departed to a solitary place; and there He **prayed"*** (Mark 1:35). Prayer was such a priority to Jesus that he got started *"a long while before daylight"*—probably before anyone else was awake and could distract Him.

+ **An open heaven and the Father's affirmation.** *"When all the people were baptized, it came to pass that Jesus also was baptized; and while He prayed, the heaven was opened. And the Holy Spirit descended in bodily form like a dove upon Him, and a voice came from heaven which said, 'You are My beloved Son; in You I am well pleased'"* (Luke 3:21–22). Wouldn't you like to have this kind of experience today, hearing Father God speak to you from heaven to affirm His love for you as His beloved child? Prayer is the key.

+ **The power of the Holy Spirit to do miracles.** *"Then Jesus returned in the power of the Spirit to Galilee"* (Luke 4:14). This happened immediately after Jesus had spent 40 days of prayer and fasting, and immediately before a wonderful season of ministry and miracles.

+ **Divine direction.** *"Now it came to pass in those days that He went out to the mountain to pray, and continued all night in prayer to God. And when it was day, He called His disciples to Himself; and from them He chose twelve whom He also named apostles"* (Luke 6:12–13). Jesus recognized the importance of choosing the right people as His inner core of disciples, and He spent "all night in prayer to God" before making His decision.

+ **Revelation and salvation to others.** *"And it happened, as He was alone praying, that His disciples joined Him, and He asked them, saying, 'Who do the crowds say that I am?' So they answered and said, 'John the Baptist, but some say Elijah; and* *others say that one of the old prophets has risen again.' He said to them, 'But who do you say that I am?' Peter answered and said, 'The Christ of God'"* (Luke 9:18–20). This is one of the pivotal passages in the gospels, where Peter has a supernatural revelation of Jesus' identity as the Messiah. But don't miss the fact that Jesus was *"alone praying"* immediately before this event happened. Do you have unsaved friends and loved ones who don't yet have an understanding of who Jesus is? You can be confident that as you pray for them, God will open their eyes.

+ **Transformation.** *"He took Peter, John, and James and went up on the mountain to pray. As He prayed, the appearance of His face was altered, and His robe became white and glistening"* (Luke 9:28–29). Although your prayers may not result in a dramatic *transfiguration* like this, they definitely will result in a transformation of your life, as you become more and more like Christ. Paul wrote of this in 2 Corinthians 3:18: *"We all, with unveiled face, beholding as in a mirror the glory of the Lord, are being transformed into the same image from glory to glory, just as by the Spirit of the Lord."*

+ **Restoring those who have fallen.** *"The Lord said, 'Simon, Simon! Indeed, Satan has asked for you, that he may sift you as wheat. But I have prayed for you, that your faith should not fail; and when you have returned to Me, strengthen your brethren'"* (Luke 22:31–32). Jesus predicted that Peter would deny Him; but because of His prayers, Jesus also was confident that Peter would ultimately be restored.

Isn't it amazing how much importance Jesus placed on prayer as a key to unlocking His power and authority? The disciples noticed this, and they wisely asked Jesus, *"Lord, teach us to pray"* (Luke 11:1). We have no record of them asking Him how to preach, heal the sick, or cast out demons, but they recognized that prayer was the secret to all these other spiritual activities.

Perhaps you would say to me today, "Pastor Caldwell, I've tried praying for what I need, but it just doesn't seem to work." Well, friend, Jesus anticipated your question. Whenever He urges us to *pray*, He also mentions the need for *persistence*: *"Jesus told his disciples a parable to show them that they should always **pray and not give up**"* (Luke 18:1 NIV).

Don't give up, my friend. Your breakthrough will come, but you need to persevere in your prayers: *"Ask, and it will be given to you; seek, and you will find; knock, and it will be opened to you"* (Luke 11:5–13).

Turbocharge Your Prayers by Fasting

Remember the time when Jesus' disciples were unsuccessful in casting out a demon from a young boy? (See Mark 9:16–29.) Jesus explained to the puzzled disciples, *"This kind cannot come out by anything but prayer and fasting"* (Mark 9:29).

Many early texts include the words *"and fasting"*, because the early church recognized the powerful effects that fasting could have their prayer lives and spiritual warfare. It's significant that Jesus Himself was fasting when He overcame the devil's temptations in the wilderness.

On a number of occasions during Jesus' ministry, prayer and fasting played a key role in releasing miracles and overcoming the devil. Immediately after His forty days of prayer and fasting at the start of His ministry, we read that *"Jesus returned in the power of the Spirit to Galilee"* (Luke 4:14).

A short time later, Jesus went into the synagogue in Nazareth and read the wonderful passage from Isaiah 61:1–3, predicting that the Messiah will be anointed to preach the gospel, heal the brokenhearted, proclaim liberty to the captives and recovery of sight to the blind, set at liberty those who are oppressed, and proclaim the acceptable year of the Lord. (See Luke 4:18–19.) Then He shocked those in the synagogue by applying this passage to Himself: *"Today this Scripture is fulfilled in your hearing"* (Luke 4:21).

Today, it's still possible to have an anointed, gospel-preaching ministry that heals the brokenhearted, sets spiritual captives free, and heals blind eyes! But we must follow Jesus' example of dedicating ourselves to prayer and fasting.

Although fasting doesn't change God, it does change us. It crucifies our flesh and allows the Spirit to gain ascendency in our lives. The combination of prayer and fasting is a powerful way to activate the authority we've been given in Christ.

Look at God's promises in Isaiah 58 regarding *"the fast that [God has] chosen"* (Isaiah 58:6):

1. Bonds of wickedness will be loosed (Isaiah 58:6)
2. Heavy burdens will be lifted (verse 6)
3. Spiritual yokes will be broken, and the oppressed will be set free (verse 6)
4. Light and healing will be released (verse 8)
5. Righteousness will be seen in our lives (verse 8)

6. God will hear and answer our prayers (Isaiah 58: 8)

7. The Lord's glory will protect us from harm (verse 8)

8. God will guide us (verse 11)

9. Our soul will be satisfied (verse 11)

10. We will be strengthened (verse 11)

11. Our life will be like a fruitful, watered garden (verse 11)

12. The *"waste places"* in our life will be rebuilt (verse 12)

Take a minute to read these great promises again and let them sink deeply into your heart. One or more of these promises will apply to whatever need you may have in your life. God wants to guide you, provide for you, satisfy you, strengthen you, and make you fruitful for His kingdom!

16

THERE'S POWER IN THE BLOOD

Even if you employ all the other principles of spiritual authority, it's critical that you don't overlook the power you've been given through the blood of Jesus. Remember: You're not called to stand in your *own* authority to defeat the enemy. It's all about standing in *Jesus'* authority; and the blood signifies the covenant relationship you have with Him.

Describing the devil as *"the accuser"* (Revelation 12:10) thrown down to earth in the last days, Revelation 12:11 provides a surefire strategy for victory over him:

They overcame him because of the blood of the Lamb and because of the word of their testimony, and they did not love their life even when faced with death.

Do you see why Jesus' blood is such a crucial weapon in our arsenal against Satan? It's the seal of our salvation, the proof of our forgiveness, and the sign of our covenant relationship with almighty God! The devil's accusations are nullified whenever we apply the blood of Jesus to our warfare.

The blood of Jesus is referred to as *"the blood of the **Lamb**"* (Revelation 12:11). The Bible reveals Jesus as *"the Lamb of God who takes away the sin of the world"* (John 1:29), and His shed blood is foreshadowed in the Feast of the Passover:

> *Then the whole assembly of the congregation of Israel shall kill* [the Passover lamb] *at twilight. And they shall take some of the blood and put it on the two doorposts and on the lintel of the houses where they eat it....For I will pass through the land of Egypt on that night, and will strike all the firstborn in the land of Egypt, both man and beast; and against all the gods of Egypt I will execute judgment: I am the LORD. Now the blood shall be a sign for you on the houses where you are. And when I see the blood, I will pass over you; and the plague shall not be on you to destroy you when I strike the land of Egypt.*
> (Exodus 12:6–7, 12–13)

Passover is a beautiful illustration of the supernatural protection you have when you apply the blood of Jesus to the doorposts of your heart, your mind, your body, your family, your finances, and every other aspect of your life. Apply the blood of Jesus over your life...

+ when the thief comes to steal, kill, and destroy;

+ when the devil comes as a roaring lion, seeking someone to devour;

+ and when demons of sickness, poverty, lust, addiction, fear or depression look for someone to prey upon.

They will have to pass over you and find someone else to attack!

Although preaching on "the power of the blood" isn't very fashionable these days, the Bible says it is important, for *"without shedding of blood there is no forgiveness"* (Hebrews 9:22 NASB). This theme of the shedding of blood has been described as a "scarlet thread" that extends throughout the entire Bible, from Genesis to Revelation.

It's interesting that Rahab the harlot was saved by tying a *"cord of scarlet thread"* (Joshua 2:18 NASB) to the window of her house. Though everyone else in Jericho was killed in battle, she and her family were kept safe by the scarlet cord! (See Joshua 2:17–21.) Similar to the Passover blood on a family's doorposts, this scarlet cord represents the protection we have from evil because of the blood of our Passover Lamb—Jesus.

Rahab's salvation wasn't based on her own virtue or righteousness—she was a prostitute, after all! Her only hope for safety was the scarlet cord that kept her safe from attack.

I encourage you to take a few minutes to pause and pray. Make sure *"the blood of the Lamb"* (Revelation 12:11) has been applied to every area of your life. Be certain you aren't basing your relationship with God on your own goodness but on the "scarlet cord" that testifies of Jesus' death on your behalf.

Other Prongs of the Formula

In addition to *"the blood of the Lamb,"* Revelation 12:11 mentions *"the word of [our] testimony"* as one of the key weapons we have to defeat Satan. As Solomon warns, our words are powerful, either for good or for evil: *"Death and life are in the power of the tongue, and those who love it will eat its fruit"* (Proverbs 18:21). In spiritual warfare, boldly proclaiming God's faithfulness is a potent way to set the devil running.

This is another principle of warfare exemplified by David. When naysayers tried to discourage him from fighting Goliath, David responded with words of faith:

> *"Your servant has killed both lion and bear; and this uncircumcised Philistine will be like one of them, seeing he has defied the armies of the living God." Moreover David said, "The Lord, who delivered me from the paw of the lion and from the paw of the bear, He will deliver me from the hand of this Philistine."* (1 Samuel 17:36–37)

David first testified to God's faithfulness in the *past,* helping him to overcome a lion and a bear. Then he proclaimed his confidence in God's *present* help in defeating Goliath.

When David confronted Goliath—who was roughly twice his size—the giant belittled him and cursed him by the Philistine gods. But David continued to speak words of faith and victory:

> *Then David said to the Philistine, "You come to me with a sword, with a spear, and with a javelin. But I come to you in the name of the Lord of hosts, the God of the armies of Israel, whom you have defied. This day the Lord will deliver you into my hand, and I will strike you and take your head from you. And this day I*

*will give the carcasses of the camp of the Philistines to the birds of the air and the
wild beasts of the earth, that all the earth may know that there is a God in Israel.
Then all this assembly shall know that the* LORD *does not save with sword and
spear; for the battle is the Lord's, and He will give you into our hands."*

(1 Samuel 17:45–47)

David saw that Goliath's weapons were only effective in the physical realm: a
sword, a spear, and a javelin. In contrast, David knew that he battled with a far more
powerful weapon: *"the name of the* LORD *of hosts."* Perhaps Paul had this story in
mind when he wrote that the weapons of our warfare are not *"carnal"* (2 Corinthians
10:4) or *"of the flesh"* (NASB) but mighty through God.

What a great portrait of our warfare against the hordes of hell! We don't need
weapons that depend upon our own strength, for *"the battle is the Lord's"* (1 Samuel
17:47).

If you are struggling in your battle against the enemy today, I encourage you
to take a look at the words that are coming out of your mouth. Words of faith are a
mighty weapon to defeat Satan; words of doubt, fear, and unbelief will simply play
into the enemy's hands and bring about your defeat.

The Final Ingredient

The victorious believers described in Revelation 12:11 displayed one final component of successful warfare: *"They did not love their lives to the death."* In other words,
there wasn't any question about whose side they were on!

In contrast, many Christians today are living defeated lives because of *compromise.* Although they claim to follow Christ, they still have one foot planted in Satan's
kingdom! However, compromised lives like this violate a cardinal principle of spiritual authority: *"If a kingdom is divided against itself, that kingdom cannot stand"* (Mark
3:24). Victory comes only when our hearts are undivided and our faith is not mixed
with unbelief!

I encourage you today to check your heart and see if you've compromised in
some way and allowed the devil to gain entrance into your life. How can you defeat
Satan if you're secretly harboring areas of darkness in your life; if you've given the
devil a foothold through the TV shows or movies you watch or the songs you listen
to or the Internet sites you visit or the books and magazines you read?

You may not be able to stop all of Satan's attacks, but you surely can keep him from gaining victory over you. As someone once observed, "You can't keep the devil from flying over your head, but you can keep him from building a nest in your hair!" Remember: Before the devil will flee from you, you first must submit yourself fully to God. (See James 4:7.)

The Lord hasn't planned any defeats for you! When you model your life after the threefold formula in Revelation 12:11, you can be confident of a triumphant life in Christ:

> *Thanks be to God, who always leads us in triumph in Christ, and manifests through us the sweet aroma of the knowledge of Him in every place.*
>
> (2 Corinthians 2:14 NASB)

This victorious life is God's will for you! Draw near to Him today, and learn to use the powerful weapons He's given you for victory.

17

THE AUTHORITY IN
YOUR HAND

As a pastor, I've often encountered Christians who complain about what they don't have. "Pastor Caldwell," they whine, "my life would be so much better if I just had more money." Or they grumble that God hasn't given them enough time or enough talent.

My standard reply to such people is to ask, "What have you done with what you *do* have? Has everything been given back to God?"

At that point, they usually squirm and stammer, admitting that they've not fully surrendered their time, talent, and treasure to the Lord. Instead, they've chosen to excuse themselves by focusing on what they didn't have. And with their focus on their lack, they ended up hoarding their meager resources out of fear.

Many of the Bible's greatest heroes were extremely wealthy, and they *all* learned to be generous with what God had given them. This is the powerful law of seedtime and harvest, found throughout God's Word. (See Genesis 8:22.)

Abraham

In Genesis 14, Abraham's nephew Lot was taken captive by enemy armies, along with his family and his possessions. When Abraham heard the news, he immediately gathered more than three hundred men to mount a counterattack.

Look at the result of Abraham's raid against the enemy forces: *"So he brought back **all** the goods, and also brought back his brother Lot and his goods, as well as the women and the people"* (Genesis 14:16).

What a great outcome! Although the enemy came as a thief, the counterattack recaptured everything that was stolen.

But the story didn't end there. After Abraham recovered the spoils of battle, he freely gave Melchizedek *"a tithe of all"* (verse 20). Melchizedek was *"the priest of God Most High"* (verse 18), and he was an Old Testament picture of Christ.

Then the king of Sodom tried to give Abraham the other spoils to keep, but Abraham refused. (See Genesis 14:21–22.) Why? Because he didn't want anyone to say that they had made Him rich. You see, he trusted God as his source and recognized the Lord as *"Possessor of heaven and earth"* (Genesis 14:19). He understood that because God was a generous, covenant-keeping God, he could be generous in sowing his resources into God's kingdom.

God had told Abraham from the beginning that He would bless him and make him a blessing:

> *I will **bless you** and make your name great; and you shall **be a blessing**. I will bless those who bless you, and I will curse him who curses you; and in you all the families of the earth shall be blessed.*   (Genesis 12:2–3)

Abraham somehow grasped the principle that when he gave the Lord what was in his hand, the Lord would then freely give Abraham what was in His hand. Instead of being an impoverished vagabond, roaming out in the wilderness, *"Abraham was very rich in livestock, in silver, and in gold"* (Genesis 13:2). And as a result of his generous lifestyle, we're told that at the end of Abraham's life, *"[he] was old, well advanced in age; and the LORD had **blessed** [him] **in all things**"* (Genesis 24:1).

Wouldn't you like this to be the testimony of your life as well? Then exercise your faith, and give God whatever He has put in your hand.

Isaac

Abraham's son Isaac followed in his footsteps in learning the laws of prosperity. He demonstrated his trust in the Lord and his understanding of the principle of seedtime and harvest when he sowed seeds even in a time of great famine:

> *Isaac **sowed** in that land, and **reaped** in the same year **a hundredfold**; and **the Lord blessed him**. The man **began to prosper**, and **continued prospering** until he became **very prosperous**; for he had **possessions** of flocks and **possessions** of herds and a great number of servants. So the Philistines envied him.*
> (Genesis 26:12–14)

This short passage is filled with vital lessons for someone who wants to gain the authority of a believer in the area of finances. Isaac didn't wait for the economy to improve before he started trusting God for his provision. No, he decided to take a step of faith and sow seeds even in that dry land.

Although we sometimes have to wait patiently for our harvest, we see that Isaac *"reaped in the same year."* Your financial turnaround can come relatively quickly, my friend. But you'd better get started *now* in planting some seeds!

For some financial investments in today's economy, you would be happy just to get your money back. Yet when Isaac obeyed God's leading and sowed seeds, he received a *hundredfold* return. Try finding an investment in the stock market that can match that kind of return!

Then look at how God's abundance continually increased in Isaac's life:

+ The Lord *blessed* him.

+ He *began* to prosper.

+ He *continued* to prosper.

+ He became *very* prosperous, so much so that *"the Philistines envied him."*

This amazing progression of blessing all started when Isaac took a step of faith to release the seeds from his hand into God's hand. He could have grumbled about the famine or complained that he didn't have more seeds to start with. But he exercised his faith instead.

Moses

Things weren't going very well for Moses and the people of God, who were living as slaves in Egypt. However, a pivotal turn of events happened in Exodus 4:2–4:

The LORD said to [Moses], "What is that in your hand?" He said, "A rod." And He said, "Cast it on the ground." So he cast it on the ground, and it became a serpent; and Moses fled from it. Then the LORD said to Moses, "Reach out your hand and take it by the tail" (and he reached out his hand and caught it, and it became a rod in his hand).

At first, this may have seemed like a rather insignificant miracle. Moses was told to lay down a shepherd's rod. It became a snake but then returned to its original shape when Moses reached down and grabbed it again. So what's the big deal?

My friend, something powerful happens whenever we give God what is in our hand. The shepherd's staff was merely a simple piece of wood in Moses' hand, but after he laid it down, it was transformed into *"the rod of God"* (Exodus 4:20).

Quite a transformation took place, all because Moses gave God what was in his hand. The rod may have *looked* the same, but now it was full of God's power and authority. Moses was able to use the rod in miraculous ways:

+ To bring judgment on the Egyptians (Exodus 9:23, 10:13)
+ To part the Red Sea (Exodus 14:16)
+ To bring gushing water out of a rock (Exodus 17:5–6)
+ To defeat enemy armies (Exodus 17:8–13)

The moral of the story is this: You may not feel like you have much in your hand right now, but God can do great things if you give Him the little that you have.

Samson

Samson, an important figure in the book of Judges, had an up-and-down life. Despite his magnificent calling, he sometimes disobeyed the Lord, and the consequences were often disastrous.

One day when a large band of Philistines came against Samson, *"the Spirit of the LORD came mightily upon him"* (Judges 15:14). There were hundreds of these enemy warriors, and Samson seemingly had no weapons. Guns hadn't been invented, and he had nothing like a sword, slingshot, or bow and arrow. So what could he do?

With the Lord's Spirit upon him, Samson came up with a very creative solution: *"He found a fresh jawbone of a donkey, reached out his hand and took it, and killed a thousand men with it"* (Judges 15:15). Think of it: One thousand Philistine men were slain with the jawbone of a donkey! Just as we've already seen with Abraham, Isaac, and Moses, the Lord can do great things if we let Him use what is in our hand.

David

No one saw young David as a giant killer. He was just a shepherd boy, without any military training or experience. However, David had learned to trust God while taking care of his father's sheep. And although he had never battled a giant like Goliath before, he had rescued the sheep from lions and bears, as he explained to King Saul. (See 1 Samuel 17:34–37.)

David had learned to be "faithful in little things" (see Luke 16:10), and God entrusted him with a *big* thing—defeating a very *big* giant. David had no confidence in Saul's armor or in any of the weapons used by the Israelite soldiers. Instead, he used the weapon God had already placed in his hand: a slingshot and a stone.

Yet the real key to David's victory was that he understood the *authority* he had when he stood in the name of the Lord. Take a look again at what he told Goliath:

> *You come to me with a sword, with a spear, and with a javelin.* **But I come to you in the name of the Lord of hosts,** *the God of the armies of Israel, whom you have defied.* (1 Samuel 17:45)

What a great example for us in how to defeat the "giants" in our life. We must engage the enemy based on our authority *"in the name of the Lord of hosts"* and then allow God's Spirit to use the resources or weapons He has placed in our hands.

A Boy's Lunch

Massive crowds were following Jesus from place to place, and they were getting hungry. (See John 6:5–13.) The disciples opted for the simple solution: Dismiss the crowd and send the people away.

Jesus wanted to *feed* the hungry crowd, but this seemed like an impossible option. The only resources they could find were clearly inadequate: *"There is a lad here who has five barley loaves and two small fish, but what are they among so many?"* (John 6:9).

However, God is never concerned about the *size* of the seed in your hand or whether it appears adequate to meet the need. He just wants you to give the resources to Him!

How many people could have been fed by these meager resources under normal circumstances? One or two? Maybe three? But when this boy's small supply of food was placed in Jesus' hands and blessed by Him, thousands of hungry people were fed! Even more remarkable, the disciples were able to gather up twelve full baskets of *leftovers*. What a testimony to the kind of overflowing abundance God intends for His people!

What's In Your Hand?

God never requires what we don't have, but He *does* expect us to freely surrender what we *do* have. He can multiply seeds during a time of famine, turn a simple shepherd's staff into the rod of God, use the jawbone of a donkey to slay thousands of the enemy, or kill huge giants with a slingshot and a stone. And it's no problem for Him to multiply loaves and fish, feeding an enormous crowd and providing an abundant supply of leftovers.

However, miracles like this can't begin until you put your resources—no matter how meager they may seem—into His outstretched hands. The authority, power, and provision you need is not far away, but right there in your hand!

18

BATTLE STRATEGIES

As discussed in the previous chapters, God has given us overwhelmingly powerful weapons in the name of Jesus, along with the Scriptures, prayer, and the resources He has placed in our hands. However, none of these weapons will do us any good unless we use them.

King David gave thanks to God for preparing him for victory in battle: *"Blessed be the Lord my Rock, who trains my hands for war, and my fingers for battle"* (Psalm 144:1). Just as David discovered, the Lord is eager to equip us with everything we need for success in the Christian life and victory over the enemy.

However, victory isn't automatic just because we're saved. We must take time to learn God's prescribed battle strategies and become familiar with our spiritual armor and weapons. Then we must go on the *offensive* against any stronghold of the devil in our life or the lives of our loved ones.

Remember: We will never appropriate God's promises and His power by being passive. Even if you know who you are in Christ, you'll never move any "mountains" if you fail to exercise that authority. Passivity has crippled many Christians and many churches; so you must shake off any tendencies in that direction. God has called you to be a mighty warrior in Jesus' name!

Jesus' Example

You've probably watched movies or seen paintings of Jesus with long, flowing hair and rosy cheeks—pretty effeminate, to say the least. Yet the *real* Jesus wasn't a wimp or a pacifist. He was a man's man, with unlimited boldness, power, and authority.

Notice how Jesus handled a demon He encountered in the synagogue one day:

> *Now in the synagogue there was a man who had a spirit of an unclean demon. And he cried out with a loud voice, saying, "Let us alone! What have we to do with You, Jesus of Nazareth? Did You come to destroy us? I know who You are; the Holy One of God!" But Jesus rebuked him, saying, "Be quiet, and come out of him!" And when the demon had thrown him in their midst, it came out of him and did not hurt him. Then they were all amazed and spoke among themselves, saying, "What a word this is! **For with authority and power He commands the unclean spirits, and they come out.***" (Luke 4:33–36)

People mentioned two key words when they saw Jesus deal with this situation: "*authority and power.*" Authority involves having the right or authorization to use power. As part of His original creation, God authorized Adam to take dominion and exercise authority over everything He had made.

Although Satan has *power* to steal, kill, and destroy, he doesn't have *authority* to do so. He doesn't have any authority to inflict you and your family with sickness. Yes, he has power to come and attack us, but as a believer, you have authority to resist him and make him flee.

Just as Jesus simply rebuked the demons, we can exercise that same authority. The people who gathered in the synagogue marveled at Jesus' authority, just as people will marvel when *we* take authority in His name. Sadly, many Christians are waiting for Jesus to heal them or rebuke the enemy, but all the while, Jesus has delegated that authority to us as believers. (See Luke 10:19.)

Six Strategies for Victory

We've already established that God willingly delegates His authority to believers—but that's the easy part. The harder part is for us to *believe* and *exercise* the authority we've been given. This requires a boldness that is rarely exhibited by

Christians today. No wonder Jesus once asked, *"When the Son of Man comes, will He really find faith on the earth?"* (Luke 18:8)

I've discovered six scriptural keys to *activating* our authority as believers:

1. Fight the good fight of faith.

Make no mistake about it: You'll never destroy enemy strongholds without a fight! And this fight must be carried out with faith, as Paul told Timothy:

Fight the good fight of faith, lay hold on eternal life, to which you were also called and have confessed the good confession in the presence of many witnesses.
(1 Timothy 6:12)

This charge I commit to you, son Timothy, according to the prophecies previously made concerning you, that by them you may wage the good warfare, having faith and a good conscience, which some having rejected, concerning the faith have suffered shipwreck. (1 Timothy 1:18–19)

Faith is a law; faith is a spirit; and faith is also a fight. In order to succeed in the life of faith, you must be willing to fight the flesh and the devil. Yes, the battle is the Lord's, but we have to fight the fight.

2. Resist the devil.

Satan won't run away from you unless you actively resist him, as James tells us: *"Submit to God. Resist the devil and he will flee from you"* (James 4:7). Resisting isn't something you can do passively; it requires action. In order to exercise your authority as a believer, you must use God's Word as a sword to expose and defeat the devil's lies.

3. Overcome evil with good.

In order to defeat evil, you must replace it with good. Darkness is only dispelled by the presence of light. Hate can only be defeated by love. Again, overcoming requires action rather than passivity. You will never overcome obstacles, grief, sickness, poverty, strife, or anything else by just sitting down and giving up. The Bible teaches that evil will overcome us if we don't overcome it first! So let's rise up and fulfill our calling as overcomers: *"Do not be overcome by evil, but overcome evil with good"* (Romans 12:21).

Years ago, I read an article about the difference between babies born naturally through the birth canal and babies born by C-section. I realize that sometimes a C-section is medically necessary, but the babies that are born that way have a disadvantage. Babies delivered by C-section don't have to go through the normal struggles of being born. When a baby is born naturally, he or she has to *fight* and *struggle* to get through the birth canal. They are getting their first experience in being an overcomer!

Not long ago, a US Army general was asked his thoughts about the present generation of soldiers. On the one hand, he said they were highly intelligent and had great communication skills. But he expressed sadness that they tended to be the laziest and most unfocused generation he had ever seen.

You may not agree with the general's assessment, but I think there's some truth in what he said. In many cases, the generation we're now raising has never had to struggle for anything. They feel entitled to an easy life, and every imaginable convenience has simply been handed to them. Because of this, they've often missed out on life's struggles that develop character and "stick-to-it-iveness."

4. Be fervent in prayer.

We must aggressively pursue God for the things we need in prayer. Paul illustrated this necessity with a woman travailing in childbirth: *"My little children, for whom I labor in birth again until Christ is formed in you"* (Galatians 4:19). Instead of polite, passionless prayers, we're told, *"The effective, fervent prayer of a righteous man avails much"* (James 5:16). This doesn't promise that all prayers avail much— just prayers that are *"effective"* and *"fervent,"* offered from a *"righteous"* person. This doesn't imply emotionalism or "squalling and bawling," which is usually accompanied by unbelief. It means that you must stand boldly on God's promises and exercise your authority as a believer.

5. Work hard.

People of faith should also be people who believe in hard work. Faith is a key ingredient for success, but *"faith without works is dead"* (James 2:26). That's why Peter wrote, ***"Make every effort** to respond to God's promises"* (2 Peter 1:15 NLT). God has given us great promises, but we must make a *diligent effort* to respond to them in faith. Personally, I believe that every young man should have to do some hard physical labor early in life. It would also help them to serve in the military to learn discipline and hard work. Such things build not only muscles, but character.

6. Pull down enemy strongholds.

Satan has declared war on you, so you sometimes must openly declare war on him. As well as declaring war on the devil for what he's trying to do you and your loved ones, you can declare war on things like drugs, alcohol, profanity, and pornography. Again, this is a matter of action rather than passivity, but Paul reminds us that it's fundamentally a spiritual battle that we're engaged in:

> We are human, but we don't wage war as humans do. **We use God's mighty weapons**, not worldly weapons, **to knock down the strongholds** of human reasoning and to destroy false arguments. We destroy every proud obstacle that keeps people from knowing God. We capture their rebellious thoughts and teach them to obey Christ. (2 Corinthians 10:3–5 NLT)

Years ago, the Playboy Channel was trying to become an addition to the cable system in our city, and a throng of Christians went down to meet with the city board of directors. We filled up the city board room, and an overflow of people lined up outside and down the sidewalk.

We were there to tell the board members, "You may have the legal authority to do this. But we are standing up to put you on notice that if you allow the Playboy Channel to air on our TVs, it will destroy the spiritual climate and moral fabric of this city. You have been given authority to make decisions for the people of this city, but the consequences also rest on your shoulders."

Despite our pleas, the board voted to pick up the Playboy Channel. However, after being on the cable channel for one year, it went broke and went off the air. And it hasn't been on since.

Notice the important lesson here: You won't always see the victory right away, but you must stand up and wage the good warfare nevertheless. Winston Churchill famously said it this way: "Never give in. Never give in. Never, never, never, never—in nothing, great or small, large or petty—never give in, except to convictions of honor and good sense. Never yield to force. Never yield to the apparently overwhelming might of the enemy."

Toward the end of his life, the apostle Paul was still fighting the fight of faith: *"I have fought the good fight, I have finished the race, I have kept the faith"* (2 Timothy 4:7). What a great legacy! Paul didn't quit pursuing his mission until it was completed. Paul modeled fighting the good fight, and this is why he wrote to Timothy about faithfully waging spiritual warfare.

Activating Your Authority

Your authority as a believer is not just a nice theory—it's a settled truth. However, your authority will do you absolutely no good unless you put it into *action*.

It shouldn't surprise us, then, that Jesus wasn't primarily a theoretician or theologian. Instead, He was a man of action. Here's just a small glimpse of how Jesus took action to heal people, perform miracles, cast out demons, and feed the hungry multitudes:

- He cast the legion of demons out of the mad man. (Mark 5:1–13)
- He spoke to the fig tree, and it withered. (Matthew 21:18–20)
- He healed the blind man with clay and spittle. (John 9:1–7)
- He spoke to the storm, and it was calmed. (Mark 4:35–39)
- He commanded His dead friend Lazarus to come back to life, and he did. (John 11:38–44)

It's time to follow Jesus' example and put your authority into action. Speak to the obstacles and "mountains" in your life. Rebuke the enemy and tear down his strongholds. Boldly step into your Promised Land!

19

TAKING BACK WHAT THE ENEMY HAS STOLEN

When I teach on our authority as believers, there's often someone in the congregation who tells me, "Pastor Caldwell, I'm grateful for your message. But I wish I had heard it many years ago. The devil has stolen my health, my finances, and my children, and now it's too late to do anything about it."

If this is how you are feeling today, I have good news for you: Through the authority found in Jesus' name, God can enable you to take back what the enemy has stolen from you!

Yes, the devil is a thief, and he comes *"to steal, and to kill, and to destroy"* (John 10:10). He hates God, and he hates the people of God. He's a liar, and he wants you to think there's nothing you do about the things he has stolen. If you listen to these lies, you will feel depressed and hopeless. But in the next few pages, I will share *truth* that will set you free! (See John 8:32.)

If you are feeling ripped off by the devil in some area of your life, you are certainly not alone. Many of the Bible's greatest heroes faced times when their enemies stole from them. However, God enabled them to mount a counterattack and recapture what was lost!

In Genesis 14, Abraham's nephew Lot was taken captive by enemy armies, along with his family and his possessions. When Abraham heardthe news, he immediately gathered more than three hundred men to pursue the enemy.

Look at the result of Abraham's counterattack: "*So he brought back **all** the goods, and also brought back his brother Lot and his goods, as well as the women and the people*" (Genesis 14:16).

I love this story! Although the enemy came as a thief, the counterattack recaptured everything that was stolen. So don't lose heart, my friend. God is planning a turnaround for *you*, as well.

David's Breakthrough

David faced a similar situation in 1 Samuel 30:1–9. When he and his men came to Ziklag, they discovered thatthe Amalekites had invaded the town and taken their wives and children captive. This was such a horrible situation that the men "*lifted up their voices and wept, until they had no more power to weep*" (1 Samuel 30:4). Perhaps you are experiencing a time of weeping in your life today, much like these men. If so, remember God's great promise: "*Weeping may endure for a night, but joy comes in the morning*" (Psalm 30:5).

Sometimes it's difficult to wait for the victory. David became "*greatly distressed*" (1 Samuel 30:6), particularly when his men spoke of stoning him! Yet David was a man after God's heart, and he knew where his strength came from: "*David strengthened himself in the* LORD *his God*" (1 Samuel 30:6).

If Satan has stolen something that belongs to you, my friend, you need to follow David's example and find hope and strength in the Lord's presence. But notice that after strengthening himself in the Lord, David didn't stop there. He took another vital step toward his ultimate victory: "[He] *inquired of the* LORD" (1 Samuel 30:8). When you're facing spiritual attack, nothing is more important than seeking God's strategy for a counterattack. You can't allow yourself to just sit on your sofa and worry. You need to have an action plan—a comeback strategy that is born out of prayer.

When David discovered the enemy's attack, he didn't remain passive. Nor did he wallow in defeat or allow the enemy to keep what was stolen. After David prayed and got his bearings, he immediately went on the *offensive* and prepared his counterattack.

War in the natural realm is a violent and bloody endeavor, and spiritual war isn't much different. When David discovered the enemy encampment, he wasn't in the mood to compromise or negotiate: *"David attacked them from twilight until the evening of the next day. Not a man of them escaped, except four hundred young men who rode on camels and fled"* (1 Samuel 30:17).

David's counterattack was an aggressive act of war, which is the same kind of spirit we must have to overcome the powers and principalities of the devil. Jesus observed that *"the kingdom of heaven suffers violence, and the violent take it by force"* (Matthew 11:12). Victory is available in Jesus' name, but we have to throw timidity aside!

The beautiful thing about David's counterattack is that it wasn't primarily about taking *revenge* against the enemy. Instead, it was focused on recapturing everything that had been stolen:

> *So David recovered **all** that the Amalekites had carried away, and David rescued his two wives. And **nothing of theirs was lacking**, either small or great, sons or daughters, spoil or anything which they had taken from them; **David recovered all**.* (1 Samuel 30:18–19)

This should be your vision today as well. Recover *all* that the enemy has stolen from you. Instead of accepting defeat or feeling like a victim, it's time to grasp your authority in Christ and go on the offensive!

Receiving Double for Your Trouble

As wonderful as it is to recover what the enemy has taken from us, often the Lord wants to give us *more* than that. We see this in the Old Testament laws that required a thief to pay back even more than what he stole.

> *If a man steals an ox or a sheep, and slaughters it or sells it, he shall restore **five** oxen for an ox and **four** sheep for a sheep.* (Exodus 22:1)

> *If a man delivers to his neighbor money or articles to keep, and it is stolen out of the man's house, if the thief is found, he shall pay **double**.* (verse 7)

This principle is wonderfully demonstrated in the story of Job. Although Job was a godly man, Satan had stolen everything he had: his family, his health, and his possessions.

But even in a fierce spiritual battle like Job's, the enemy's attacks weren't the end of the story! God broke through in Job's life and gave him even more than he had lost: "*The* LORD *restored Job's losses....Indeed the* LORD *gave Job* **twice as much as he had before**" (Job 42:10). Job literally was given *double* for all his *trouble*!

Let your faith be strengthened by this today. If Satan has ripped you off in some way, there's no need to get stuck in a "victim" mentality. God wants to bless you, restore what you've lost, and give you even more than you started with!

Restoring the Years

Some people have been victimized by the enemy for so long that their feelings of victimhood have become a "familiar spirit," deeply ingrained in their hearts and minds. Instead of just losing a spiritual battle or two, they feel as if they have already lost the war.

If you've entertained this defeatist mentality, God has a new beginning for you today! He's able to restore even *years* of losses from the enemy. The Bible is filled with stories of people who had suffered a long time before they exercised faith for their breakthrough. The woman with the hemorrhage had endured her condition for *twelve long years* before she touched Jesus' garment and received her healing. (See Mark 5:25–34.) The man Jesus healed in John 9:1–7 had been blind *from birth*, and the paralyzed man in John 5:2–9 had suffered from his infirmity for *thirty-eight years*. So no matter how long you may have suffered, it's not too late for your miracle!

In the days of the prophet Joel, the people of Judah faced several years of devastating attacks on their crops by locusts. Because these attacks were both severe and long-lasting, it was easy for them to lose hope:

> *What the chewing locust left, the swarming locust has eaten; what the swarming locust left, the crawling locust has eaten; and what the crawling locust left, the consuming locust has eaten....He has* **laid waste** *my vine, and ruined my fig tree; he has* **stripped it bare** *and* **thrown it away;** *its branches are made white.*
>
> (Joel 1:4, 7)

Perhaps the attacks of the enemy have left you feeling much like this today: *laid waste, ruined, stripped bare,* and *thrown away.* But God knows about your situation and wants to restore everything you've lost:

> **I will restore** to you **the years** *that the swarming locust has eaten, the crawling locust, the consuming locust, and the chewing locust.*   (Joel 2:25)

I think these are three of the most beautiful words in the English language: "*I will restore.*" God doesn't say He "may" restore or He will "try to" restore—He says He *will* restore. When you stand in your identity in Christ and your authority as a believer, you can count on it. And when the Lord says He will restore what you've lost, this means that a life of incredible blessing and abundance can await you:

> *The threshing floors shall be* **full** *of wheat, and the vats shall* **overflow** *with new wine and oil....You shall eat in* **plenty** *and be* **satisfied**, *and praise the name of the* Lord *your God, who has dealt wondrously with you; and My people shall never be put to shame.*   (Joel 2:24, 26)

Let's Get Personal

These stories from Scripture are not some kind of far-off fairy tales. They are meant to instruct and encourage believers. If the devil has stolen something from you, don't just give up and assume it's gone forever. Remember what God did for His people in His Word:

+ Abraham recovered *everything* that the enemy stole from Lot.
+ David recovered *everything* that the enemy stole from Ziklag.
+ God's law says that a thief must pay back even *more* than what he stole.
+ Job was blessed with *double* of everything Satan had stolen from him.
+ In the book of Joel, God promised to restore to us even *years* of the enemy's plunder.

Has the devil stolen something from your life. Your health? Your marriage? Your children? Your job? Your finances? Your vision? Your peace of mind?

If so, take a moment and commit that area of your life to the Lord. Remember your position and authority in Christ, and ask Him to give you His strategy for overcoming the enemy's attacks. Take Him at His word that He will reverse your losses and bless you beyond your wildest dreams!

20

OVERCOMING EVIL SPIRITS

I n the Bible, we learn that there are different kinds of demonic spirits, and the good news is this: By our authority in Christ, we can prevail over *any* kind of spirit associated with Satan.

However, one of the first keys of warfare is that we must "know our enemy." Nations at war invest vast amounts of money and manpower to research the strategies and vulnerabilities of the nations opposing them. In our case, it's not so difficult, because the Bible already contains our "rules of engagement." It exposes the tricks of our adversary and clearly presents the tactics we must employ for victory.

Actually, the battle over Satan has *already been won*. Through our authority as believers, we are merely *enforcing* the victory Jesus purchased long ago through His cross and resurrection.

The devil is like an inner-city slumlord who has managed a high-rise apartment building for many years. The place is hellish to say the least, with rampant violence, theft, and drug abuse. The horrific conditions have lasted so long that no one exhibits hope of things ever changing.

But then the property is purchased by a *new* landlord, who is loving, kind, and just. To everyone's amazement, this landlord paid a *huge* price for this shoddy building, and He wanted everyone to know that He was serious about the "new management" that was about to occur.

The first order of business of the new landlord is to evict the squatters and evildoers. Although He is the rightful owner, with a full title deed to the property, He still has to *enforce* His ownership.

My friend, this is where you and I come into the story. Jesus is the new landlord, who has paid an enormous price to redeem the earth and its inhabitants back to Himself. However, the devil still has squatters who won't leave without being evicted—and that often requires a *fight*. We haven't been given our authority as some kind of decoration or trophy for our mantle; it's given to us so we can do battle against the enemy!

The Enemy's Roster

If you competed in a wrestling tournament, track meet, or other sports event, you might want to study the list of participants on the opposing team. Likewise, the Bible describes your opponents well and tells you how to defeat each one:

+ **Evil spirits** (see 1 Samuel 16:14–23, 18:10, 19:9): These evil spirits *"terrorized"* (1 Samuel 16:14 nasb) Saul and caused him to think irrationally. Although he sincerely loved David at times, the evil spirits caused Saul to fly into a rage and try to kill David. Luke 7:21 says that Jesus *"cured many of infirmities, afflictions, and evil spirits"*; and people were touched by this same kind of ministry by the church in Acts: *"The diseases left them and the evil spirits went out of them"* (Acts 19:12).

+ **Lying spirits** (see 1 Kings 22:21–23): While the Holy Spirit is described as *"the Spirit of truth"* (John 14:17, 15:26, 16:13), it's fitting that Satan's spirits would be characterized by lies and deception. Paul warned that in the last days, many people would be swayed by *"deceiving spirits and doctrines of demons"* (1 Timothy 4:1). And the apostle John contrasts *"the spirit of truth and the spirit of error"* (1 John 4:6).

Familiar spirits (see Leviticus 19:31, 20:6, 27; Deuteronomy 18:11; 1 Samuel 28:3, 7–9; 2 Kings 21:6, 23:24; 1 Chronicles 10:13; 2 Chronicles 33:6; Isaiah 8:19, 19:3, 29:4): In the first passage, Leviticus 19:31, the King James Version translates the Hebrew words for this spirit as *"mediums and familiar spirits,"* and the *New American Standard Bible* translates them as *"mediums and spiritists."* These foul spirits apparently are related to spiritualism and fortune-telling.

+ **Spirits of heaviness, despair, fainting, or depression:** In a wonderful example of the "great exchange" offered to us as believers, Isaiah 61:3 says God wants to replace the tormenting spirit of heaviness with *"the garment of praise."*

+ **Unclean spirits** (see Zechariah 13:2; Matthew 10:1, 12:43; Mark 1:23–27, 3:11, 30, 5:2-14, 6:7, 7:25; Luke 4:33–36, 6:18, 8:29, 9:42, 11:24; Acts 5:16, 8:7; Revelation 16:13, 18:2): As in the case of the Gadarene demoniac in Mark 5:2–14, these demons often are described as actually inhabiting and possessing their human victims.

+ **Spirits of infirmity or sickness:** This is mentioned in Luke 13:11–13 as the cause of a woman's illness. Until Jesus set her free, she was crippled for eighteen years by *"a spirit of infirmity"* (Luke 13:11). This is translated by the *New American Standard Bible* as *"a sickness caused by a spirit"* and by the *English Standard Version* as *"a disabling spirit."*

+ **Spirits of fear or timidity:** Paul refers to a spirit of fear in 2 Timothy 1:7, making it clear that such a spirit is not from God. Instead of fear and timidity, God wants to give *"us a spirit of power and of love and of a sound mind."*

+ **Spirits associated with pagan gods and idolatry** (see Leviticus 17:7; Deuteronomy 32:17; 2 Chronicles 11:15; Psalm 106:19–39; 1 Corinthians 10:20–21): Hosea 5:4 and other passages describe going after other gods as succumbing to *"the spirit of harlotry."*

+ **Principalities ruling over specific territories or geographical areas:** Daniel 10:10–21 provides one example of these powerful satanic forces that exert an influence over specific countries or regions.

The Bible describes many other kinds of evil spirits. Anger, hatred, lust, prejudice, confusion, and every other evil manifestation in human flesh, can be the direct result of demonic influence. But through God's Word and the discernment provided to us by the Holy Spirit, we don't have to be ignorant of the schemes of the enemy. (See 2 Corinthians 2:11.)

Jesus' Name Makes the Difference

Some people feel intimidated when they hear of Satan's evil army. However, such feelings play right into the enemy's hands. When we stand in our authority in the mighty name of Jesus, there's absolutely no reason to be afraid!

Jesus has given us His name as a "badge" of delegated authority. When we submit to Him and act in His name, all the power and resources of heaven are at our disposal. No enemy can stand against us when we're truly submitted to Him and grasp the awesome authority we've been given. We may not look very impressive or strong on the outside, but that's not important. In Jesus' name, we've been given a mighty badge of delegated authority.

Behind every policeman is the entire police force. Behind the FBI and National Guard stand the branches of the entire armed forces of the United States. The badge of delegated authority is far more important than an individual officer's personal strength or power.

But remember: Using our "badge" and speaking "in Jesus' name" must be more than a mere ritual, formula, or magical incantation. The devil isn't frightened by our words if they aren't based on our loving, obedient relationship with God.

His Authority Is Our Authority

Many Christians acknowledge that Jesus has great authority, but they still can't grasp the fact that *His* authority is *their* authority! So they go around discouraged and defeated, wondering why Jesus doesn't intervene in their circumstances. Yet the whole time, they have all the authority they need to speak to their circumstances and "move mountains" in Jesus' name. (See Matthew 17:20.)

Jesus prayed to the Father, *"As You sent Me into the world, I also have sent them into the world"* (John 17:18). Do you see how powerful this statement is? God sent His Son to earth for a clear objective: *"For this purpose the Son of God was manifested, that He might destroy the works of the devil"* (1 John 3:8). The *"works of the devil"* are the consequences of sin that entered the world through the disobedience of Adam and Eve: sin, sickness, relationship conflicts, and death.

Jesus was given *"all authority"* (Matthew 28:18) to accomplish His mission, and that very same authority has now been given to *us*! Jesus has sent us in the same way His Father sent Him (see John 20:21), and this means we have *all* the authority that was delegated to Christ!

Frankly, this is pretty hard for most of us to believe. Why? It's not because it isn't plainly taught in Scripture; no, we struggle to understand our full authority in Christ because it seems so contrary to our *experience*! In essence, we are saying, "I'll *believe* it when I *see* it," while God is saying, "When you start *believing* it, you'll start *seeing* it!"

So don't let Satan scare you from boldly fulfilling your mission and entering the Promised Land God has ordained for you. The Lord is bigger than any "giant" that seems to block your way. Because you've been given the authority of Christ, there's no enemy that can stand against you when you pursue your destiny in His name!

21

AUTHORITY IN THREE REALMS

My friend Charles Capps points out that we have authority in three different worlds or realms: authority in heaven, authority on the earth, and authority under the earth. Let me explain.

When Paul declared that Jesus' name is above every other name, he listed three specific groups of people who will bend their knees before Him: *"those who are in heaven, and on earth, and under the earth"* (Philippians 2:10 NASB). These are the three areas where Jesus has authority. And through His name, *we* have authority in each of these realms as well.

We have authority in heaven, because we are seated together with Christ in heavenly places. (See Ephesians 2:4–6.) Jesus told us, *"Assuredly, I say to you, whatever you bind on earth will be bound in heaven, and whatever you loose on earth will be loosed in heaven"* (Matthew 18:18).

I'm always amazed when I meet people who don't believe in a literal heaven or hell. Heaven is a real place. Hell is a real place. And the good news for believers is that when we die, we are immediately *"absent from the body and...present with the Lord"* (2 Corinthians 5:8).

Daniel chapter 10 provides a fascinating glimpse of the spiritual warfare that occurs in the heavenly places. Daniel devoted himself to prayer and fasting for three straight weeks, with no apparent results. Finally, an angel appeared to him and said,

> *Do not fear, Daniel, for from the first day that you set your heart to understand, and to humble yourself before your God, your words were heard; and I have come because of your words. But the prince of the kingdom of Persia withstood me twenty-one days; and behold, Michael, one of the chief princes, came to help me, for I had been left alone there with the kings of Persia.*　　(Daniel 10:12–13)

The angel was sent *"from the first day"* that Daniel had set himself to pray. Although Daniel didn't see the answer manifested immediately, it was on the way! What a great example of our need to persevere in prayer, knowing that God has already set things in motion to answer our request. My friend, we have authority in heaven, even when we don't see the breakthrough right away.

Daniel's prayers didn't bounce off the ceiling—they were heard in heaven! Likewise, we're told in Revelation 5:8 that, in heaven, there are *"golden bowls full of incense, which are the prayers of the saints."* However, I don't think that means that *all* prayers make it to heaven. Some prayers are merely religious gobbledygook, prayed in unbelief.

But when we pray in faith and stand on our authority in Jesus' name, we can be confident that God has heard us. From the moment we humble ourselves and pray, as Daniel did, our answer will be dispatched from heaven: *"Your words were heard; and I have come because of your words"* (Daniel 10:12).

Authority over the Earth

We have God's delegated authority on earth, because that was part of His original design for humanity. (See Genesis 1:26–28.) Jesus won that authority back for us when He *"disarmed principalities and powers"* and *"made a public spectacle of them"* (Colossians 2:15). However, we must enforce Jesus' authority on earth through our words, actions, and prayers. That's why Jesus told us to pray, *"Your kingdom come. Your will be done on earth as it is in heaven"* (Matthew 6:10).

As God's representatives on earth, we should always pray that the same will He's expressed in heaven will also be done on earth. There is no disease, poverty, depression, or strife there, my friend! Through our lives as believers, God wants the power of His heavenly kingdom to tear down enemy strongholds and supernaturally touch the world with signs and wonders that reveal His love.

I love the Moffatt translation of Philippians 3:20, which says we are *"a colony of heaven on earth."* When people see our lives, they should catch a glimpse of God's heavenly kingdom. And He has prescribed very clear keys for unleashing His kingdom authority on the earth. These include such things as binding and loosing, seedtime and harvest, and speaking to "mountains" in Jesus' name.

Yet many Christians are waiting to get to heaven before they start exercising their faith and claiming their victory. However, you won't need to bind and loose anything up there. You won't need to cast out any demons up there. You won't need to lay hands on the sick up there. But you *do* need to employ these weapons in your spiritual warfare here on earth.

Authority over Hell and Death

The final realm where we have authority is hell, depicted as *"those under the earth"* (Philippians 2:10). Just as Jesus has authority in heaven and on earth, He told the apostle John that He also has *"the keys of hell and of death"* (Revelation 1:18 KJV).

Instead of referring to some kind of material keys that would unlock hell or Hades, Jesus was talking about *authority* in this passage. Jesus wanted to make sure John understood that He had overcome death, hell, and the grave, and that He had taken the keys (authority) back from Satan. As a result, believers have authority over hell and death. You can live without fear, as we are told to do in Hebrews 2:14–15:

Because God's children are human beings—made of flesh and blood—the Son also became flesh and blood. For only as a human being could he die, and only by dying could he break the power of the devil, who had the power of death. Only in this way could he set free all who have lived their lives as slaves to the fear of dying.
(NLT)

Isn't this wonderful? Jesus now has the keys to death and hell, for He broke *"the power of the devil, who had the power of death."* As believers, we no longer need to live *"as slaves to the fear of dying."* Satan was our jailer, but Jesus has stolen his keys and set us *free!*

Enforcing Jesus' Victory

Jesus won the victory for us, but we must stand in His delegated authority in order to enforce that victory on the earth. The devil still has a vast network of demons that seek to do us harm if we're willing to let them.

Whenever I teach on the subject of spiritual authority, I try to make it clear that while not everything is a demon, there are many human circumstances that are, in fact, demonic. When we face difficult situations and conflicts, we have to be able to discern whether an evil spirit is at work.

The Bible says, *"We do not wrestle against flesh and blood, but against principalities, against powers, against the rulers of the darkness of this age, against spiritual hosts of wickedness in the heavenly places"* (Ephesians 6:12). This means that *people* are not our enemies, even though it's possible for them to be used either by God or by Satan.

Demons are disembodied spirits. They have no bodies of their own, so they seek to embody any humans who will open the door for them. If they're unable to get into humans, they will take over an animal, such as a horse, dog, or pig. Have you ever seen a demon-possessed horse? If you want to rent a horse to ride and are given one named Diablo, don't get on that horse! Other animals can be possessed, as well. I once saw a demon-possessed dog who was two hundred pounds of demonic power.

Demons use people, and God uses people. Sometimes demons will use people and situations to attack you, and that's why the gift of discerning spirits is so important. You need to know what's coming against you so you can stand against it. Jesus said you have authority *"over all the power of the enemy, and nothing shall by any means hurt you"* (Luke 10:18). But this doesn't work well if you don't even recognize that the devil is the one attacking you.

Too often, Christians naïvely think that their troublesome situations just happen randomly, like a coincident or an accident. Don't be fooled! There are demonic forces trying to steal, kill, and destroy from God's people. (See John 10:10.) If sickness, depression, financial lack, relationship conflict, or some other situation is coming against you, know that it's not from God! And you have the power and authority to command it to leave. As Jesus' disciples discovered, *"the demons are subject to us"* (Luke 10:17) through His name.

Do you remember the story of Paul being bitten by a poisonous snake while picking up a bundle of sticks? (See Acts 28:1–6.) Not worried at all, Paul simply shook off the snake into the fire. Expecting him to die from the snake bite, the onlookers were amazed when he wasn't impacted in the least. In the same way, people are watching you and me, my friend. When they see that we're overcomers, not succumbing to Satan's attacks, they will have to recognize that God is real.

But remember: The authority God has delegated to you doesn't make you immune to the enemy's attacks. It just gives you power to overcome them. But because of your position in Christ, you can be confident that you have authority in heaven, authority on earth, and even authority to overcome the powers of hell.

22

PERFECT SUBMISSION, PERFECT AUTHORITY

The centurion in Matthew 8:5–13 understood that Jesus could demonstrate extraordinary authority over sickness and situations because He was in perfect submission to the Father. But many Christians don't really comprehend what submission involves.

To submit oneself means to surrender to the authority, discretion, will, or judgments of another person. If you submit to someone's authority, you are surrendering to their instruction, correction, and decisions. The main Greek word for "submit" is *hypotassō* and includes the following meanings:

1. to arrange under, to subordinate

2. to subject, put in subjection

3. to subject one's self, obey

4. to submit to another person's control

5. to yield to another person's admonition or advice

Submission isn't a popular topic for most people today. Many of us have an independent streak, and we don't like the thought of someone telling us what to do. This is particularly true in America, where we're proud of our right to do things our own way. Too often, submission is seen as something negative or demeaning, but nothing could be further from the truth.

For a believer who expects to walk in authority, it's absolutely essential to submit to God's authority and the delegated authorities He has put over us. Jesus is our perfect model on this, so let's look at some examples in His life.

Jesus' Submission to the Father

Many people are very surprised when they learn that Jesus never spoke or acted on His own authority. Though He was the Messiah and God's Son, He submitted Himself to His Father's leading on every occasion.

> *Most assuredly, I say to you, the Son can do nothing of Himself, but what He sees the Father do; for whatever He does, the Son also does in like manner.*
>
> (John 5:19)

> *I can of Myself do nothing. As I hear, I judge; and My judgment is righteous, because I do not seek My own will but the will of the Father who sent Me.*
>
> (John 5:30)

> *Do you not believe that I am in the Father, and the Father in Me? The words that I speak to you I do not speak on My own authority; but the Father who dwells in Me does the works.*
>
> (John 14:10)

Isn't this rather astounding? If Jesus did nothing on His own initiative, we certainly should be careful to submit *our* words, thoughts, and actions to the Father, as well.

Jesus' submission to the Father wasn't based on some kind of low self-image. Quite the contrary, He originally existed *"in the form of God,"* and He *"did not consider it robbery to be equal with God"* (Philippians 2:6). This meant Jesus didn't think it took away from His deity to become humanity. He maintained both divinity and humanity at the same time.

Nevertheless, He *"made Himself of no reputation, taking the form of a bondservant, and coming in the likeness of men. And being found in appearance as a man, He humbled Himself and became obedient to the point of death, even the death of the cross"* (Philippians 2:7–8).

Jesus' submission to His Father's will was not partial, but total. He displayed *unconditional* surrender and obedience, *"to the point of death, even the death of the cross."* Because of this perfect submission, Jesus was granted the ultimate place of authority:

> **Therefore** God also has highly exalted Him and given Him the name which is above every name, that at the name of Jesus every knee should bow, of those in heaven, and of those on earth, and of those under the earth, and that every tongue should confess that Jesus Christ is Lord, to the glory of God the Father.
>
> (Philippians 2:9–11)

Notice the word *"therefore"* in this passage. Jesus was *"highly exalted"* because He first humbled Himself. What a great model this is for us. As Jesus taught His disciples, *"Whoever exalts himself will be humbled, and he who humbles himself will be exalted"* (Luke 14:11).

Too often, people forget this. They fail to understand that we must learn to humble ourselves and submit to authority if we're going to exercise authority. Perhaps you've met people like this. They mistakenly assume that "walking in authority" means trying to "be somebody." So they start walking around with an arrogant, unteachable spirit, refusing to receive instruction or repent when they are wrong.

Not Our Will, But His Will

Sometimes people *claim* to have a submissive heart, when their attitudes and actions are quite the contrary. They may seem fine when everyone agrees with them, but when someone crosses them, they suddenly become stubborn, angry, and rebellious.

When there is true submission to authority, *our* will is submitted to God's will and to the delegated authorities He has placed over us. The *test* comes when God tells us something we don't want to hear!

Again, Jesus is our perfect example of what to do in such a situation:

> He went a little farther and fell on His face, and prayed, saying, "O My Father, if it is possible, let this cup pass from Me; nevertheless, not as I will, but as You will."
>
> (Matthew 26:39)

Jesus certainly didn't relish the idea of being brutally beaten and then nailed to a cross until He died by suffocation, all the while bearing the sins of world. Even so, the main goal of His prayer was not to get the Father to spare Him. Rather, He wanted to make sure He was fully submitted to the Father's will.

But notice that Jesus did not pray, "If it be Your will." A lot of times, Christians negate their prayers and their faith by adding "if it be Your will" at the end of their request for healing, provision, or something else they need from God. This usually is a very misguided way to pray. Why? Because we have a remarkably simple way to find out God's will on most subjects. He has already told us what to do in His Word!

In order to fully align Himself to the Father's will, Jesus had to be willing to lay down His life:

Therefore My Father loves Me, because I lay down My life that I may take it again. No one takes it from Me, but I lay it down of Myself. I have power to lay it down, and I have power to take it again. This command I have received from My Father. (John 10:17–18)

No one could kill Jesus or take His life. He *voluntarily* laid down His life in submission to the Father's will. This attitude characterized Jesus all the way until His last breath on the cross: *"Father, 'into Your hands I commit My spirit'"* (Luke 23:46).

Jesus' Place of Authority

Having made the ultimate act of submission to the Father's authority, Jesus was given the ultimate place of honor, with authority over all of creation. Paul tells the Ephesian believers that after raising Jesus from the dead…

[God] seated Him at His right hand in the heavenly places, far above all principality and power and might and dominion, and every name that is named, not only in this age but also in that which is to come. And He put all things under His feet, and gave Him to be head over all things to the church, which is His body, the fullness of Him who fills all in all. (Ephesians 1:20–23)

My friend, this passage isn't just about Jesus; it's about you and every other believer who is a part of His body. If you understand your identity in Christ, you'll see that your authority is tied together with His. You are seated with Him in heavenly places, far above all demonic and earthly powers. (See Ephesians 2:6–7.)

I encourage you to take a few minutes now and meditate on this great truth about your union with Christ and the incredible authority you've been given in Him. Whatever problems you're facing are miniscule in light of His overwhelming power and authority. You can give thanks *"to Him who is able to do exceedingly abundantly above all that we ask or think, according to the power that works **in us**"* (Ephesians 3:20). Victory is at hand!

23

A RENEWED MIND

In order to grasp the authority we have as believers in Christ, we all need to have our minds renewed. Whether from our childhood, our church background, or the secular culture in our nation, we've all picked up some "stinkin' thinkin'" that is contrary to what God's Word says about our new identity in Christ.

The Bible makes it clear that when you were born again, you became a *"new creation"* in Christ. Your former life is gone, for the *"old things have passed away; behold, all things have become new"* (2 Corinthians 5:17).

However, Satan will try to do what he can to bring you back down to the old negative mind-set you had before you got saved. He'll tell you how unworthy you are and remind you of past failures and criticisms people have made about you. Perhaps you were raised in a home where your parents repeatedly said you would never amount to anything. The prisons are full of men and women who were told all their lives that they were destined for a life of failure, just like their daddy, older sibling, or some other family member. Seeds of failure were planted in their heart, and these seeds grew into self-fulfilling prophecies.

Fortunately, God can intervene in people's negative circumstances and transform their lives. The changes are not automatic, and they may not happen all at once.

Paul says in Roman 12:1–2 that we must first present ourselves to God as a *"living sacrifice"* (Romans 12:1) and then allow Him to renew our mind by His Word.

It is impossible to walk in God's authority unless our minds have been renewed. Part of what it means to be in submission to the Lord is *coming into agreement* with what He says about us in Scripture. If the Bible says you are *"the righteousness of God in* [Christ]" (2 Corinthians 5:21), but you say you're "just a dirty old sinner saved by grace," you still haven't fully aligned yourself with God's truth.

Our righteousness in Christ is part of our inheritance in the Great Exchange. For our sake, He accepted every one of our weaknesses and liabilities, so that we might become like Him, empowered by His mighty strength and ability. Jesus became sin so we could become the righteousness of God in Him (see 2 Corinthians 5:21), but that was just the beginning. He took upon Himself our sicknesses so that we could be healed. (See 1 Peter 2:24.) He took our poverty so that we might experience His wealth. (See 2 Corinthians 8:9.) And He bore our griefs and sorrows so we could receive His incredible peace. (See Isaiah 53:4–5.) Hallelujah!

This is no small matter. Unless we understand what happened in the Great Exchange Jesus won for us at the cross, we will never see ourselves correctly. And we're told in Proverbs 23:7, *"As he thinks in his heart, so is he."* This means we will *become* what we *think about ourselves*.

What about you, my friend? Do you see yourself as God sees you, through the eyes of His covenant and His grace? If not, it's time to renew your mind and change the way you think!

A New Mind-set

Having your mind renewed will impact your decisions and behavior. There's simply no way to make the right choices if your mind-set is all wrong.

For example, if you grew up in America and then moved to Great Britain, you would have to change your mind about which side of the road to drive on. You could protest that it's not an important issue or claim that you should be able to drive on whichever side of the road you preferred. But it would be *dangerous* to be wrong in your thinking on this!

You also would have to get used to the steering wheel located on the other side of the car. It wouldn't do you much good to ask a car mechanic to move the steering wheel to the side you're used to. You simply must *submit* and have your mind renewed on the subject of how to drive in Great Britain.

Just as you would need a new mind-set in order to drive successfully in Great Britain, you will require a new way of seeing things once you enter into the life of a believer. You'll have to remember that you are not the same person anymore. It may take some time for your mind to be adjusted to start thinking like God thinks. But it's part of the process Paul was describing when he said, *"Let this mind be in you which was also in Christ Jesus"* (Philippians 2:5).

Let's face it: We live in a very rebellious, self-centered, self-willed world today. Think of all the lawsuits that are caused simply because many folks refuse to humble themselves and submit to anyone. Even Christians often struggle to fully yield to the Lord and to His Word.

However, submission is not an optional part of the Christian life! In fact, it is the starting point of true discipleship. In order to walk in spiritual authority, we must take Jesus' words seriously and apply them to our lives: *"If anyone desires to come after Me, let him deny himself, and take up his cross daily, and follow Me"* (Luke 9:23).

Let these words sink in for a moment. Are you denying yourself, taking up your cross daily, and truly following Jesus? This is the road to discipleship—and the gateway to spiritual authority.

A Surprising Key to God's Favor

One of the clearest indications of whether we're truly submitted to God is whether we are honoring His delegated authorities in our life. We see this principle at work in God's prescription in the Ten Commandments: *"Honor your father and your mother, that your days may be long upon the land which the LORD your God is giving you"* (Exodus 20:12). While the first commandments deal with idolatry and serving other gods, the commandment to honor our parents is, when considered honestly, a "reality check" about whether we've truly committed ourselves to God.

As a child, Jesus submitted Himself to His earthly parents, Mary and Joseph. (See Luke 2:42–52.) He had *first* submitted Himself to God, and He told His parents, *"Did you not know that I must be about My Father's business?"* (Luke 2:49). But the story ends with a clear depiction of Jesus honoring and obeying His parents:

He went down with them and came to Nazareth, and was subject to them, but His mother kept all these things in her heart. And Jesus increased in wisdom and stature, and in favor with God and men. (Luke 2:51–52)

This short passage is full of powerful applications. Immediately after the statement about Jesus subjecting Himself to the delegated authority of His earthly parents, we're told of four fantastic blessings He received: (1) He increased in wisdom; (2) He increased in stature; (3) He increased in favor with God; and (4) He increased in favor with other people. All these blessings were released after He willingly submitted to His parents. God took Him to a *higher* place of favor after He humbled Himself and *"went down with them."*

Wouldn't you like to increase in wisdom and favor? The surprising key may be to submit to God's delegated authorities in your life.

Modeling Authority to Your Children

Many Scripture passages teach children to honor and obey their parents. (See Exodus 20:12; Ephesians 6:1–2; Colossians 3:20.) Fathers and mothers are God's delegated representatives in the home. Children may not always like this, but it is how God designed things.

We violate God's divine order at our own peril. Part of His blueprint for the home is that our relationships model honor and respect, and we should willingly submit to the delegated authority He has established. Following God's instructions is a command, not just an option. You can trace most of society's ills back to rebellion, self-will, and discipline problems in the family.

Of course, some parents have taken their authority too far. They've bought into the misconception that they must "break the will" of their child. This is not what the Scriptures teach. Yes, children should be taught to *yield* their will to the parents, but this doesn't imply that the parents should bring discipline out of anger or an abusive spirit.

One of the most important things a parent can do for their child(ren) is simply to *model* a respect for authority. If we could fix that in our families today—instilling honor and respect once again—we could eliminate the vast majority of problems in our culture. But it begins with parents following the biblical example—raising their children in the nurture and admonition of the Lord. (See Ephesians 6:4.)

There will always be people who say, "Times have changed. We can't expect the same level of respect from our children anymore." Yes, times have changed. We definitely have a different cultural climate than when I was raised. But although society is different today, biblical principles are the same—and they still work when we apply them.

Colossians 3:20 says, *"Children, obey your parents in all things, for this is well pleasing to the Lord."* Sometimes, people misapply this truth, saying that children should always obey parents who are drunkards, drug addicts, abusive, or involved in illegal or immoral activities. However, that's not what Paul is saying here. Our obedience to God and His Word comes *before* our obedience to our parents or any other kind of delegated authority. Children are called to obey their parents in all things that are godly and biblical, not in things that are evil and immoral.

Trusting God's Delegated Authorities

Throughout the Scriptures, we're given instructions about the need to submit to the human authorities God has placed over us. Sometimes this is extremely difficult. The key ingredient is trust, but even Jesus Himself was careful about not trusting Himself to just anyone: *"Jesus would not entrust himself to them, for he knew all men. He did not need man's testimony about man, for he knew what was in man"* (John 2:24–25 NIV).

So, if people are inherently imperfect and unreliable, how are we supposed to submit to them or trust them? The key is that we must *first* entrust our lives to the Lord, as shown by Peter's instruction to wives about submitting to their husband:

> *In the same way, you wives must accept the authority of your husbands....This is how the holy women of old made themselves beautiful. **They trusted God and accepted the authority of their husbands**. For instance, Sarah obeyed her husband, Abraham, and called him her master. You are her daughters when you do what is right without fear of what your husbands might do.*
>
> (1 Peter 3:1, 5–6 NLT)

Peter illustrates that the key to accepting the husband's authority—or any delegated authority, for that matter—is to first put our trust in God. He cites Sarah as a great example of this principle. Do you remember the times Abraham told people that Sarah was his "sister," and she was taken into the king's harem?

(See Genesis 12:10–20, 20:1–18.) It wasn't always *easy* for Sarah to submit to Abraham! But she put her trust in the Lord, and everything turned out all right in the end.

In the final analysis, submission to delegated authority is all about *trust*. If children have a trust relationship with their parents, it's easy to obey and submit to them. You've probably watched as a toddler jumped off the side of a swimming pool into the arms of his father or mother. And although he trusts his parents to catch him, he might be reluctant to jump into the arms of a stranger.

The same is true of our submission to our heavenly Father. It's all about trust. If we really do trust Him, we should be able to obey what He says, even if we don't understand it. If we're confident that He loves us and has a great plan for our lives, we will gladly submit our decisions to Him.

Friend, if you're struggling to entrust your life fully to God today, I encourage you to spend time reading and meditating on His Word. Open your heart wide to the Lord again and ask the Holy Spirit to fill you. The more you spend time with Him, the more your trust will grow.

Trusting God isn't just some kind of religious jargon; it's extremely practical, affecting every area of our lives. We need to learn to trust God with our health, our money, our marriages, our kids, and many other things.

What happens if you have a medical examination and receive a bad report? Will you allow your heart to be gripped with fear or will you trust God to heal you? The X-ray may indicate a very real problem, but God has a *different* report. As the prophet Isaiah asks, "*Who has believed our report?*" (Isaiah 53:1). We must choose life, and choose to believe the report of the Lord.

Over the years, I've also had to learn to trust God with my finances. The reason so few Christians tithe is that they don't really trust the Lord with their money. When I started tithing, it didn't seem to be working at first. There simply didn't seem to be enough money. But when I asked God about it, He told me, "Just trust Me and keep doing it." That was forty years ago, and He has never failed to provide for me. My trust in Him is greater today than it has ever been before.

Because I've learned to trust God with my health, finances, and other areas of life, I am able to walk in *God's authority* in those areas. As the old hymn says so well, "Trust and obey, for there's no other way to be happy in Jesus, but to trust and obey!"

24

HEAVEN'S REPRESENTATIVES ON EARTH

All authority has to have a source and a location. Of course, we know that God is our ultimate source, and it's critically important that we understand where our authority comes from.

For instance, if you attempt to return an item to a store, you generally must have the receipt. That receipt proves where you purchased the item and your right to possess it or return it. If someone at the store challenges your authority to return the product, the receipt establishes your right by proving the item's source. The same is true of our spiritual authority: It's critical that we know its source and location.

Likewise, if you purchase a car or appliance that comes with a warranty, you have to read the fine print to know exactly what the authority of that warranty covers. In the same way, you need to read and study God's Word to find out exactly what your authority covers and how you can operate in it.

Years ago, when Jeanne and I first launched Agape Church, a lady asked me by whose authority I had started the church. Her query shocked me at first, and all I could think to say was, "By *Jesus'* authority!" However, that answer did not satisfy her.

"You don't understand," she continued. "What *man* gave you the authority to start this church?"

I thought for a moment and replied, "Well, Jesus is a man, and He gave us the authority."

"No, no, you still don't understand," she insisted. "What man who is alive today gave you permission to start this church?"

I answered again, as politely as I could, "Well, ma'am, Jesus is a man. He is definitely alive today, and He still is starting churches."

As you can imagine, this still didn't satisfy her. Although I knew beyond a shadow of a doubt that my authority was located in Jesus, this wasn't good enough for her. She wanted me to reduce the location of my authority to some human source, but I had confidence to stand my ground and declare where my authority came from. Instead of coming from some human organization or denomination, my authority had been derived from my position seated in the heavenly places in Christ. (See Ephesians 2:4–6.)

Overcomers

God wants us to be overcomers. If we truly understand that we're seated with Christ in the heavenly realms—*far above* any spiritual power that could ever come against us—we've already taken a huge step toward a life of victory and blessing. We can look *down* on our problems from a place of authority.

Often, if you ask Christians how they're doing, their response will be something like this: "Pretty good, considering what I'm going through." Well, there may be problem with that kind of response. You see, there's a great lesson we can learn from Abraham, who is known as *"the father of all those who believe"* (Romans 4:11):

> *Not being weak in faith, he **did not consider his own body, already dead** (since he was about a hundred years old), **and the deadness of Sarah's womb.** He did not waver at the promise of God through unbelief, but was strengthened in faith, giving glory to God, and being fully convinced that what He had promised He was also able to perform. And therefore "it was accounted to him for righteousness."*
> (Romans 4:19–22)

While we so often love to think about, talk about, and "consider" our difficult circumstances and the obstacles we face, Abraham refused to even *consider* the fact that his own body and Sarah's womb were past the age of childbearing. What did that matter in light of God's promise to give them a son?

You might be going through difficult circumstances today, but you don't have to live under those circumstances. You are called to be an *over*-comer, seated with Christ and able to rise above your problems. Neither sin nor Satan has any authority to rule over you anymore, because they are now under your feet.

When Jesus said *"the **gates** of Hades shall not prevail against* [His church]" (Matthew 16:18), He was referring specifically to authority. Jesus was telling us that the authority of hell cannot prevail against the believing church. Since He has passed on His authority to the church, His followers can meet and overcome any of the problems they encounter in life. Whether their problems are personal, political, financial, or cultural in nature, if the followers of Christ know their authority and stand on the power of the Word, they can be confident of their victory.

This confidence is not spiritual pride. Instead of being based on some inherent goodness or ability on our part, it is derived from our position in Christ and the victory He won for us on the cross. By His death and resurrection, Jesus not only nailed our sins to the cross but also *"disarmed the spiritual rulers and authorities. He shamed them publicly by his victory over them on the cross"* (Colossians 2:15 NLT).

This is how Jesus restored authority to all those who are genuine believers, enabling us to take dominion over the affairs of life. And this revelation of our authority is one of the vital foundation stones of the church. (See Matthew 16:18–19.)

Yet it's not enough to believe in this merely as a theological concept; we must learn to *walk* in the authority Jesus has given us. If we just sit around and talk about our problems and how the devil is beating us up and chasing us around, we will surely remain defeated. Instead, we must move forward and learn to take dominion in the world as His ambassadors. (See 2 Corinthians 5:20.)

Authority to Represent Him

Jesus has given us the authority to be His personal representatives on the earth. When people quote His statement of the Great Commission—making disciples of all the nations—they typically leave out the verse that precedes it, when He said,

"All authority has been given to Me in heaven and on earth" (Matthew 28:18). You see, without receiving His delegated authority, we will never be able to fulfill our mission.

Just as an ambassador sent from the United States to another country has authority to speak on behalf of the United States, so we have been authorized to speak on behalf of God and His kingdom. We are envoys of the Lord, and we speak the Word by His authority and on His behalf. And just as an ambassador on assignment is granted immunity from any kind of prosecution, we have been given that kind of immunity from any condemnation, because of Christ's sacrifice. (See Romans 8:1.)

But I'm convinced that the reason many believers don't want to know about their authority is that they're unwilling to accept the responsibility that comes with that authority. God has given each of us gifts, talents, and abilities to further His kingdom, and we have a responsibility to use what He has given us.

Yes, with every *revelation* comes a corresponding *responsibility*. And this is certainly true when we learn about a believer's authority. We simply can't keep it to ourselves. The message is a foundational part of our duty preach the *"gospel of the kingdom…in all the world as a witness to all the nations"* (Matthew 24:14).

In addition to our responsibility to preach the gospel throughout the world, we also are called to stand guard on behalf of other believers. We must be on the lookout for attacks of the enemy; and Paul compares this to guard duty in the military:

> *Finally, my brethren, be strong in the Lord and in the power of His might. Put on the whole armor of God, that you may be able to stand against the wiles of the devil. For we do not wrestle against flesh and blood, but against principalities, against powers, against the rulers of the darkness of this age, against spiritual hosts of wickedness in the heavenly places. Therefore take up the whole armor of God, that you may be able to withstand in the evil day, and having done all, to stand…praying always with all prayer and supplication in the Spirit, being watchful to this end with all perseverance and supplication for all the saints.*
> (Ephesians 6:10, 18)

God promises to give us victory when we believe and obey Him. But we have a responsibility to do *our* part, which is to be alert, put on each item of armor, and pray.

Faithfulness Rewarded

In the parable of the talents (see Matthew 25:14–30), Jesus made it clear that each of us has been given a different amount of resources, opportunities, and natural abilities:

> *For the kingdom of heaven is like a man traveling to a far country, who called his own servants and delivered his goods to them. And to one he gave five talents, to another two, and to another one, to each according to his own ability; and immediately he went on a journey.*   (Matthew 25:14–15)

However, even though we begin at different starting points, we each are responsible for faithfully investing and multiplying whatever we've been given. God expects an *increase* in our lives, and so should we:

> *Then he who had received the five talents went and traded with them, and made another five talents. And likewise he who had received two gained two more also. But he who had received one went and dug in the ground, and hid his lord's money.*   (Matthew 25:16–18)

When we accept our responsibilities as believers to faithfully invest what God has given us, we will inevitably be rewarded:

> *After a long time the lord of those servants came and settled accounts with them. So he who had received five talents came and brought five other talents, saying, "Lord, you delivered to me five talents; look, I have gained five more talents besides them." His lord said to him, "Well done, good and faithful servant; you were faithful over a few things, I will make you ruler over many things. Enter into the joy of your lord." He also who had received two talents came and said, "Lord, you delivered to me two talents; look, I have gained two more talents besides them." His lord said to him, "Well done, good and faithful servant; you have been faithful over a few things, I will make you ruler over many things. Enter into the joy of your lord."*   (Matthew 25:19–23)

However, just as there are rewards when we faithfully exercise our authority, there is punishment for those who ignore their responsibilities:

Then he who had received the one talent came and said, "Lord, I knew you to be a hard man, reaping where you have not sown, and gathering where you have not scattered seed. And I was afraid, and went and hid your talent in the ground. Look, there you have what is yours." But his lord answered and said to him, "You wicked and lazy servant, you knew that I reap where I have not sown, and gather where I have not scattered seed. So you ought to have deposited my money with the bankers, and at my coming I would have received back my own with interest. Therefore take the talent from him, and give it to him who has ten talents. For to everyone who has, more will be given, and he will have abundance; but from him who does not have, even what he has will be taken away. And cast the unprofitable servant into the outer darkness. There will be weeping and gnashing of teeth." (Matthew 25:24–30)

God has given us so much, my friend, and there's no excuse for being an "unprofitable servant." He has given us His awesome authority, and *"His divine power has given to us all things that pertain to life and godliness, through the knowledge of Him"* (2 Peter 1:3).

We've been given the power and authority to bind and loose, heal the sick, cast out demons, and release financial blessings. We don't want to stand before the judgment seat of Christ and have Him ask us why we didn't exercise this incredible authority. It would be so sad to finally realize in eternity that we could have rid our families of sickness, received financial breakthroughs to bless our loved ones and fulfill the Great Commission, and set people free from demon spirits.

An exciting life awaits those who will believe God's promises and faithfully exercise His authority on the earth. The world desperately needs the church to arise and demonstrate the kingdom of heaven. There's no time to lose!

25

THE HUMILITY OF
TRUE AUTHORITY

When people first hear the message of a believer's incredible authority, they sometimes get the wrong idea. "Surely a person with that kind of outlook would become very arrogant," some folks say.

However, nothing could be further from the truth. Those who truly understand their authority in Christ are humble rather than arrogant. They've submitted themselves fully to the Lord and are deeply aware that they've received His authority through grace rather than through their own merit or worthiness.

Paul reminds us of Jesus' own example of humility:

*Let this mind be in you which was also in Christ Jesus, who, being in the form of God, did not consider it robbery to be equal with God, but made Himself of no reputation, taking the form of a bondservant, and coming in the likeness of men. And being found in appearance as a man, He **humbled Himself** and became obedient to the point of death, even the death of the cross. **Therefore God also has highly exalted Him.*** (Philippians 2:5–9)

This says God highly exalted Jesus because *"He humbled Himself and became obedient."* This matches other Scriptures about the proper route to God's favor: *"God opposes the proud but favors the humble....Humble yourselves before the Lord, and he will lift you up in honor"* (James 4:6, 10 NLT). Put simply, when we humble ourselves before the Lord, His favor and authority can be released in our lives.

Humility doesn't mean putting ourselves down or adopting a bad self-image. It simply means accepting what God says about us. When we look at Paul's description of Jesus' humility, an important key is that Jesus understood who He was. He didn't think it took away from His deity to be human, and He didn't believe it took away from His humanity to be God. He was fully comfortable with being both God and man.

Paul says that when we have the attitude of Christ, we'll be a willing servant of others: *"Let each of you look out not only for his own interests, but also for the interests of others"* (Philippians 2:4). Yes, we will stand boldly in Christ's authority, but we will *use* that authority to bless people's lives and show them His love.

In the following passage, Jesus gave us a very clear example of what true authority looks like:

> **Jesus knew that the Father had given him authority over everything** and that he had come from God and would return to God. So he got up from the table, took off his robe, wrapped a towel around his waist, and poured water into a basin. Then **he began to wash the disciples' feet,** drying them with the towel he had around him.
> (John 13:3–5 NLT)

Do you want to operate in your maximum authority as a believer? Then never forget this crucial principle modeled by Jesus: The more spiritual authority you have, the more you must also have a servant's heart. The Lord has given you His delegated authority, not to serve your own interests, but to represent His kingdom and humbly minister to people.

A New Kind of Leadership

While faith ensures our place of authority, only humility will retain it. Without humility, we become arrogant in our authority and proud of our revelation. Paul warned, *"Knowledge puffs up, but love builds up"* (1 Corinthians 8:1 NIV). Should we desire to grow in our knowledge and revelation? Of course, but we must take pains to grow in our love and humility, so that we use our authority properly.

Jesus repeatedly addressed this with His disciples. When James and John said they wanted to sit on His right and left hand in His kingdom, Jesus told them,

> *You know that those who are considered rulers over the Gentiles lord it over them, and their great ones exercise authority over them. Yet it shall not be so among you; but whoever desires to become great among you shall be your servant. And whoever of you desires to be first shall be slave of all. For even the Son of Man did not come to be served, but to serve, and to give His life a ransom for many.* (Mark 10:42–45)

Jesus was prescribing a whole new model of how to be a leader. Yet, too often, church leaders throughout history have sought to imitate worldly philosophies of leadership and management that are much different from what Jesus taught.

The scribes and Pharisees sadly never understood the model of a servant leader. Jesus described them in very unflattering terms:

> *All their works they do to be seen by men....They love the best places at feasts, the best seats in the synagogues, greetings in the marketplaces, and to be called by men, "Rabbi, Rabbi."* (Matthew 23:5–7)

These leaders were people-pleasers rather than God-pleasers. Their good deeds were done to impress others, they sought positions of power, and they loved being called by prestigious titles, such as *"Rabbi."*

In stark contrast, Jesus told His disciples what a kingdom leader should look like:

> *He who is greatest among you shall be your servant. And whoever exalts himself will be humbled, and he who humbles himself will be exalted.* (Matthew 23:11–12)

Before I move on to the next point, I encourage you to pause for a moment and ask yourself whether you are using your authority as a believer to serve others or just to advance your own agenda. This is a critical question. If you want to operate in Jesus' authority, you have to operate with His servant's heart. Never forget: *Kingdom leaders* must be *servant leaders.*

False Notions of Humility

As with everything, there are some people who take this principle too far and try to impress people with their humility. "I'm just a nobody," they frequently say. "I'm not seeking any glory or recognition, for I'm just a humble pilgrim trudging through life." Rather than being genuine, this is too often the result of false humility and a religious spirit.

Another common misconception is that we should pray for God to humble us. "Oh, Lord, keep us humble!" some people pray. While this may *sound* like an admirable prayer, it totally misses what the Bible teaches: *"Humble yourselves in the sight of the Lord, and He will lift you up"* (James 4:10). Do you see the difference? Instead of asking God to humble us, we are told that it is *our* responsibility to humble ourselves.

However, this verse also includes a wonderful promise. If we do what God says, humbling ourselves in His presence, He promises that *"He will lift [us] up."* So it's *our* job to humble ourselves and *His* job to lift us up. Many of us have reversed this at times, asking God to humble us and then lifting up ourselves in pride when He doesn't promote us.

The Bible also tells us that *"God resists the proud, but gives grace to the humble"* (James 4:6). So, if you sense that the Lord is resisting you today, you may need to humble yourself so that He can show you the reason.

Finally, one final misconception about humility should also be addressed: Humility doesn't imply being a wimp. It doesn't mean we should allow people to use us as a doormat. Nor does it mean we should have a low self-image and see ourselves as a second-class citizen in God's kingdom.

Genuine humility is received when we honestly and openly approach the Lord and get our validation from Him. It means thinking soberly and properly of ourselves, not thinking of ourselves as higher or lower than we really are. The bottom line is that humility enables us to think about ourselves in the same way God thinks about us.

Examples of Godly Humility

Being humble certainly doesn't imply that we should be shy or timid about using our authority as a believer. Paul told Timothy, *"God has not given us a spirit of timidity, but of power and love and discipline"* (2 Timothy 1:7 NASB). Although it may seem surprising, some of the boldest leaders throughout church history have also been the most humble. Why is this? Because boldness in believers can only be fully released when they have humbled themselves before the Lord.

In one of his crusades, Oral Roberts encountered a heckler who accused him of being proud. Think about how you would answer such a charge.

"Sir," Oral responded politely, "it is only my humility that prevents me from telling you how truly humble I really am." What a genius comment that was. Our humility in the sight of God allows us to maintain a right attitude even when unfairly accused. We're able to maintain our position and authority in Christ, without resorting to the flesh.

Humility means *knowing who God has made you*, no matter what people or circumstances may say. I absolutely love this statement in Numbers 12:3: *"Moses was very humble, more than all men who were on the face of the earth."* Do you know who wrote this commentary on Moses' great humility? *Moses did!* He knew who he was, and he wasn't shy about stating it.

Kenneth Hagin Sr. used to tell a story about a time when he was the pastor of a church in Texas. There was a deacon in the church, a precious man of God, who worked on an oil rig. One day the man fell off an oil derrick and was immediately paralyzed. When Brother Hagin was called to the hospital and saw the condition of this man whom he treasured, he went into the hallway and prayed by himself, "Lord, I need this man, and You *know* how much I need him. Therefore, I'm coming humbly and boldly, asking you to raise him up."

It was just a simple prayer, but it had the authority of God behind it. To the doctors' amazement, the man was supernaturally healed, able to resume his job and to continue his service to the church. This was another great example of the boldness and authority that can be released when we humble ourselves and pray.

Azusa Street

Humility was the foundational characteristic of the Azusa Street Revival in the early twentieth century. This incredible move of God's Spirit laid the foundation for several major denominations: Pentecostalism, the charismatic movement, and the Word of Faith movement. *Millions* of people have come into the kingdom of God as a result.

William J. Seymour was the humble man of God used to spark this world-changing revival. From 1906 to 1909, the world heard of the supernatural signs, wonders, and miracles flowing from the nightly meetings at Azusa. Blind people received their sight, sick and dying people were miraculously healed, and numerous other types of miracles were documented.

Blind in one eye, Seymour was an uneducated black man with little biblical training. His ministry in Los Angeles began at a little house on 312 Azusa Street, with seats for only about thirty people. The seating consisted of wooden planks on empty nail kegs.

During the meetings, Seymour would pray with his head down until the Spirit of God would energize him. His humble demeanor would then fall away, and he would step out in bold faith to work miracles through the power of God. A critic said, "He stays on his knees much of the time with his head hidden between the wooden milk crates. He doesn't talk very much but at times can be heard shouting 'Repent'...and he's supposed to be running the thing."

What an inspiring story of humility and world-shaking boldness. We desperately need more men and women today who will follow in William J. Seymour's footsteps and dare to exercise their authority to perform signs and wonders in Jesus' mighty name.

My friend, no matter what your situation may be today, I'm convinced that God wants to use you in a powerful way. When you humble yourself, He *will* lift you up!

26

RESPECTING CHURCH AND CIVIL LEADERS

Rebellion is a dangerous thing. King Saul learned this the hard way, when the prophet Samuel told him, *"Rebellion is as the sin of witchcraft, and stubbornness is as iniquity and idolatry"* (1 Samuel 15:23).

What an amazing statement. Those who engage in rebellion against God or His delegated authority are engaging in spiritual witchcraft. And if we stubbornly cling to our own ways instead of submitting to God, our actions are akin to iniquity and idolatry.

Miriam and Aaron were godly people, but they made a terrible mistake when they chose to rebel against the leadership of their brother, Moses:

Then Miriam and Aaron spoke against Moses because of the Ethiopian woman whom he had married; for he had married an Ethiopian woman. So they said, "Has the LORD indeed spoken only through Moses? Has He not spoken through us also?" And the LORD heard it. (Now the man Moses was very humble, more than all men who were on the face of the earth.) Suddenly the LORD said to Moses, Aaron, and Miriam, "Come out, you three, to the tabernacle of meeting!" So the three came out. Then the LORD came down in the pillar of cloud and stood in the door of the tabernacle, and called Aaron and Miriam. And they both went forward. Then He said, "Hear now My words: If there is a prophet among you, I, the Lord, make Myself known to him in a vision; I speak to him in a dream. Not so with My servant Moses; he is faithful in all My house. I speak with him face to face, even plainly, and not in dark sayings; and he sees the form of the LORD. Why then were you not afraid to speak against My servant Moses?" So the anger of the LORD was aroused against them, and He departed.

(Numbers 12:1–9)

Facing Another Rebellion

Moses certainly wasn't a perfect leader. But he was God's man, and the Lord supported him in the face of opposition. We see another example of this in Numbers 16, when Korah and 250 *"men of renown"* (Numbers 16:2) rose up against Moses and Aaron with what sounded like a legitimate accusation: *"You take too much upon yourselves, for all the congregation is holy, every one of them, and the LORD is among them. Why then do you exalt yourselves above the assembly of the LORD?"* (Numbers 16:3).

We might have expected Moses to defend himself, but he didn't. Instead, *"he fell on his face"* (Numbers 16:4) before God and told them, *"Tomorrow morning the LORD will show who is His and who is holy, and will cause him to come near to Him"* (verse 5).

Do you see how wise Moses' response was? Rather than defend himself or spend a lot of time rebuking his accusers, he humbled himself and told them the *Lord* would judge the matter. However, Moses could see that this wasn't just a rebellion against *him*—these men had *"gathered together against the LORD"* (Numbers 16:11).

Not content with just 250 followers in his uprising, Korah then *"gathered all the congregation against [Moses and Aaron]"* (Numbers 16:19). He probably felt that things were going his way at this point. Yet, blinded by his rebellion, Korah couldn't have foreseen what would happen next: *"Then the glory of the LORD appeared to all the congregation"* (verse 19).

Friend, let me point out an important lesson here. If you are causing rebellion, *beware*—the glory of the Lord may appear and rebuke you! But if you are a leader who is being wrongly attacked and accused, remember this: God will show up and *defend* you with His glory!

Moses realized that the real issue was not a conflict between human viewpoints or personalities, but rather a question of whether God had sent him, and whether he was seeking God's will. He told the malcontents: *"By this you shall know that the LORD has sent me to do all these works, for I have not done them of my own will"* (Numbers 16:28).

This story is such a great lesson in spiritual authority. Although Moses and Aaron had a rough time for a while, God ultimately vindicated them and affirmed their leadership calling. In stark contrast, things definitely did *not* end well for those who joined Korah in his rebellion. Some were swallowed up by an earthquake, while others were consumed by fire from Lord. (See Numbers 16:31–35.)

Rebellion is dangerous indeed.

Leadership in the Church

Most of the New Testament stories of rebellion aren't as dramatic as the consequences of Korah's rebellion. However, we do see the sad tale of Ananias and Sapphira falling dead when they lied to Peter about the proceeds of some land that they sold. (See Acts 5:1–11.) Again, the real issue was not lying to Peter but lying to the Lord. Peter told them, *"Why have you conceived this thing in your heart? You have not lied to men but to God"* (Acts 5:4).

As Ananias and Sapphira discovered, it's a dangerous thing to lie to the God. Perhaps they thought it was just "a little white lie" and no big deal—but it was a very big deal to the Lord.

Just as God has established delegated authority in the home, He also has put leaders in the church that deserve our support and respect. And in addition to the instruction to *"submit yourselves to your **elders** [church leaders]"* (1 Peter 5:5), we're also given a broader challenge to *"be submissive to **one another**, and be **clothed with humility**"* (verse 5). All this is in the context of God blessing those who have *humbled themselves* before Him: *"God resists the proud, but gives grace to the humble. Therefore humble yourselves under the mighty hand of God, that He may exalt you in due time"* (verses 5–6).

This passage also makes it clear that leaders in the church are to be servants, not overlords or tyrants:

Shepherd the flock of God which is among you, serving as overseers, not by compulsion but willingly, not for dishonest gain but eagerly; nor as being lords over those entrusted to you, but being examples to the flock; and when the Chief Shepherd appears, you will receive the crown of glory that does not fade away.

(1 Peter 5:2–4)

If God has called you to leadership in the church, notice what an incredible responsibility this is. One of the keys to effectively influencing people is to be an example to them of Jesus, the Great Shepherd of the sheep. People will be much more impacted by what they *see* in your life than what you *say* with your words.

Honor to Whom Honor Is Due

Honor is in short supply in our culture today. Sadly, this often is true even in the church, undermining our authority to speak as God's representatives to our communities and our nation. In order for the church to have maximum impact, it's crucial to restore our respect and honor for those in authority.

I love how *The Message* paraphrases renders these verses about the church's responsibility toward those in leadership:

Appreciate your pastoral leaders who gave you the Word of God. Take a good look at the way they live, and let their faithfulness instruct you, as well as their truthfulness. There should be a consistency that runs through us all....Be responsive to your pastoral leaders. Listen to their counsel. They are alert to the condition of your lives and work under the strict supervision of God. Contribute to the joy of their leadership, not its drudgery. Why would you want to make things harder for them? (Hebrews 13:7–8, 17 MSG)

Again we see that pastoral leaders don't just impact their flock by their teachings, but by *"the way they live,"* and this includes such things as exhibiting faithfulness, truthfulness, consistency, and accountability. In the *New King James Version*, verse 17 reads, *"Obey those who rule over you, and be submissive, for they watch out for your souls, as those who must give account."*

Notice the beautiful balance here: Leaders must be accountable to God and watch out for the souls of those they are leading. The church, in turn, is called to have an obedient and submissive attitude toward those in authority. Of course, this doesn't mean obeying leaders who counsel you to do something that is contrary to God's Word. Our first responsibility must always be to obey and submit to God Himself.

In conclusion, let me state once again how important this is to releasing God's gifts and blessings in your life. The more you recognize and receive His delegated leaders, the more He will be able to use them as a channel for His breakthroughs in your life.

As we come to an end of this chapter, take a few minutes to meditate on these powerful words from Paul to the believers in Thessalonica:

And now, friends, we ask you to honor those leaders who work so hard for you, who have been given the responsibility of urging and guiding you along in your obedience. ***Overwhelm them with appreciation and love!***

(1 Thessalonians 5:12 MSG)

27

STRANGERS IN A STRANGE LAND

I t's one thing to submit to godly authority in the home or church, but what about our obligation to respect, pray for, and submit to secular authorities? Sometimes this is extremely difficult, particularly when we vehemently oppose some of the policies of these leaders.

As Peter reminded us, *"Friends, this world is not your home"* (1 Peter 2:11 MSG). Various other translations of this verse describe believers as aliens, strangers, temporary residents, exiles, foreigners, pilgrims, or sojourners. And Paul said in Philippians 3:20 that *"our citizenship is in heaven."* So it's no wonder we often feel uncomfortable with how things are going in the political and social culture where we reside.

Nevertheless, the Bible makes it clear that, although we are citizens of the kingdom of heaven, we also have an obligation to be good citizens of wherever we live on earth. In Matthew 22:15–21, the Pharisees tried to trap Jesus with a question about whether it was lawful for God's people to pay taxes to Caesar (Rome). They thought this question would get Jesus in trouble no matter how He answered it. If He told them not to pay their taxes, the Romans would accuse Him of counseling insurrection. But if He told the observant Jews to support the despised Roman government with their taxes, they would belittle Him as a Roman sympathizer.

Recognizing the trap, Jesus said, *"Show Me the tax money"* (Matthew 22:19). He asked them whose image and inscription was on the coin, and they replied that it was Caesar's. Jesus then gave them the perfect answer to the seemingly unanswerable dilemma they had presented Him with: *"Render therefore to Caesar the things that are Caesar's, and to God the things that are God's"* (verse 21).

You see, although our primary obligation is to submit to God, He also has given us a responsibility to earthly authorities. We may not always like this arrangement, but it's something crucial for us to understand if we're going to walk in God's authority.

An Ungodly Government

Some Christians have an arrogant and disrespectful attitude toward civil government, and they typically blame their misconduct on their "submission to a higher power." Most of the time, this kind of claim is simply a rationalization for a self-willed and rebellious heart. Rather than truly being submitted to God as their "higher power," such people usually submit to *no one* but themselves.

Paul spoke at length about this issue in his letter to the Romans:

Let every soul be subject to the governing authorities. For there is no authority except from God, and the authorities that exist are appointed by God. Therefore whoever resists the authority resists the ordinance of God, and those who resist will bring judgment on themselves. For rulers are not a terror to good works, but to evil. Do you want to be unafraid of the authority? Do what is good, and you will have praise from the same. For he is God's minister to you for good. But if you do evil, be afraid; for he does not bear the sword in vain; for he is God's minister, an avenger to execute wrath on him who practices evil. Therefore you must be subject, not only because of wrath but also for conscience' sake. For because of this you also pay taxes, for they are God's ministers attending continually to this very thing. Render therefore to all their due: taxes to whom taxes are due, customs to whom customs, fear to whom fear, honor to whom honor. (Romans 13:1–7)

Paul's instruction here is particularly stunning when we consider what the Roman government was like. Many of the Roman emperors were ruthless tyrants and did not fear God!

However, Paul recognized that civil government had been originated, authorized, and endorsed by God. Because of this, Christians must look past the individual sitting in the seat of power and focus instead on God who is sitting on the throne of the universe. We have a Lord who has been placed *"far above any ruler or authority or power or leader or anything else—not only in this world but also in the world to come"* (Ephesians 1:21 NLT).

That is why we're told, *"The king's heart is in the hand of the* LORD, *like the rivers of water; He turns it wherever He wishes"* (Proverbs 21:1). Since God can change the heart of our leaders, we should pray and leave that job to Him. Paul exhorted Timothy about this important responsibility of every Christian:

> *Therefore I exhort first of all that supplications, prayers, intercessions, and giving of thanks be made for all men, for kings and all who are in authority, that we may lead a quiet and peaceable life in all godliness and reverence. For this is good and acceptable in the sight of God our Savior.*   (1 Timothy 2:1–3)

Are you praying for your President or Prime Minister, your Congress or Parliament? You should be! And as you pray, ask God to give you *His* perspective and *His* love toward those in authority. Remember: It is the "office" that God is calling you to respect and obey, regardless of the political party you voted for. Paul could not have been any clearer when he said, *"Whoever resists the authority resists the ordinance of God, and those who resist will bring judgment on themselves"* (Romans 13:2).

In the World, Not of It

Today's cultural winds in America are increasingly blowing against biblical values, and it's easy to feel exasperated, if not angry, at the way the future looks. Part of this frustration stems from forgetting that there's an inherent difference between God's kingdom and the kingdoms of this world—even the American kingdom. Even though we've been blessed because of the godly heritage received from our forefathers, we're still basically "strangers" in this world.

So, what should be our attitude toward our leaders and the country where God has placed us to live? Will we be smugly aloof, trying to keep ourselves unstained by the evil values we perceive in our society? Will we be angry and condescending, projecting an air of superiority to unbelievers? Or will we just give up and surrender, trying so hard to be accepted by the world that we end up imitating its values?

Hopefully we'll display the same attitude as Jesus displayed during His days on earth. Instead of staying aloof from unbelievers, He was known as *"a friend of tax collectors and sinners"* (Luke 7:34). He was able to be in the world without becoming absorbed by it. That's why He prayed for His followers in this way: *"I do not pray that You should take them out of the world, but that You should keep them from the evil one"* (John 17:15).

Like the Israelites who were in exile in Babylon, we often feel we're living in a strange and foreign land. But that should not be grounds for rebellion, escape, or anger. Rather, we are called to use our authority as believers, as Jesus did. Laying aside our garments of superiority, we are to pour water into a basin and "wash the feet" of our society. (See John 13:5–17.) And we're to pray for our civil leaders, whether we voted for them or not.

Finally, let's not forget to preach the gospel. In the end, that's the only way people's hearts will change and our society will be transformed.

28

OUR GREAT INHERITANCE

In order to grasp your full authority as a believer, you must see that, in Christ, God has made you His child and His heir. And among the things we've inherited is the right to use God's delegated power and authority:

> *The Spirit Himself bears witness with our spirit that we are children of God, and if children, then heirs; **heirs of God and joint heirs with Christ**, if indeed we suffer with Him, that we may also be glorified together.* (Romans 8:16–17)

We can understand this amazing truth by relating it to the legal traditions of common law. As children, we are heirs of our parents' estates when they die. In the same way, if we are children of God, then we are heirs of our spiritual Father and joint heirs with Christ.

When my father died, his will made my sister and me joint heirs of everything he owned or had authority over. Even *before* he died, he gave me power of attorney, so I had the right to conduct business in his name even while he was still alive.

When we give someone power of attorney, they have every right to use our name and carry out any legal transactions we can do. The early church understood quite well that God had given them the name of Jesus to "do business with" on the earth.

They prayed, healed the sick, raised the dead, cast out demons, and did other miracles in Jesus' name.

Doing Business in His Name

In Luke 19, Jesus told the story of *"a certain nobleman"* (Luke 19:12) who invested a substantial sum of money into the lives of his servants, telling them, *"Do business till I come"* (verse 13). In essence, these servants had the master's *power of attorney* **and** they had his *provision*. What a beautiful picture of how the Lord has invested in you and me as believers.

Of course, the perversion of this principle in our world today is identity theft. But what a contrast! With identity theft, someone uses the name of another person illegally to establish credit or do business. But when believers stand in faith to use Jesus' name, they are doing so legally, according to their great inheritance as joint heirs with Christ.

And what exactly does it mean that we are *"joint heirs"* with Christ? If a husband and wife are joint heirs of an inheritance, it means they are *equal* heirs, share-and-share-alike in the inheritance. So instead of seeing ourselves as spiritual beggars, we should be giving thanks to our Father for the great inheritance He has promised us through our covenant relationship with Christ.

When we understand our authority and inheritance as children of God, it will transform every area of our lives: our intimacy with the Lord, our health, our relationships, and our finances. However, some religious traditions teach that God is eager to punish us instead of bless us. As a result, many Christians have been led to believe that they should be afraid of God getting even with them for all the sins of their past. This warped mind-set inevitably puts people in bondage and fear.

Forgiven and Free

Make no mistake about it: Jesus paid the price so we can be free from our sins! Although that does not give us a license to continue sinning, it means God has forgiven us and has made us heirs of His kingdom. The cross is the foundation upon which we can go to God, express our repentance to Him for our sins, and receive cleansing through the blood of Jesus from all unrighteousness:

If we confess our sins, He is faithful and just to forgive us our sins and to cleanse us from all unrighteousness....My little children, these things I write to you, so that you may not sin. And if anyone sins, we have an Advocate with the Father, Jesus Christ the righteous. And He Himself is the propitiation for our sins, and not for ours only but also for the whole world. (1 John 1:9, 2:1–2)

As long as the devil can convince us we're still under the dominion of sin and condemnation, he will always have a foothold in our life. In order to exercise our authority over him, we must be absolutely persuaded that *"there is therefore now no condemnation to those who are in Christ Jesus"* (Romans 8:1).

The Bible says a person who understands God's amazing grace is *blessed* indeed: *"**Blessed** is the one whose sin the Lord will never count against them"* (Romans 4:8 NIV). The first step in being *blessed* is in knowing in your heart of hearts that you are forgiven and free.

Oh, How He Loves Us

It's crucial to understand that God doesn't just tolerate us. Nor does He just forgive us, as wonderful as that is. He *loves* us! And through the power of that covenant love, we can be assured of our victory over every enemy or difficult circumstance:

What then shall we say to these things? If God is for us, who can be against us? He who did not spare His own Son, but delivered Him up for us all, how shall He not with Him also freely give us all things? Who shall bring a charge against God's elect? It is God who justifies. Who is he who condemns? It is Christ who died, and furthermore is also risen, who is even at the right hand of God, who also makes intercession for us. Who shall separate us from the love of Christ? Shall tribulation, or distress, or persecution, or famine, or nakedness, or peril, or sword?...Yet in all these things we are more than conquerors through Him who loved us. For I am persuaded that neither death nor life, nor angels nor principalities nor powers, nor things present nor things to come, nor height nor depth, nor any other created thing, shall be able to separate us from the love of God which is in Christ Jesus our Lord. (Romans 8:31–35, 37–39)

Only by knowing God's love can we stand our ground when the enemy lies to us. Without that understanding, we'll always be vulnerable to feelings of guilt and condemnation, and it will be hard to stand in faith against attacks like sickness and poverty. Unless we have complete confidence of our forgiveness and right standing with God, our spiritual authority will be constantly undermined.

We've Got the Power!

Most Christians don't have a problem believing that God, Jesus, or even the angels have power and authority. Likewise, if they believe the Bible, they will clearly see that the early church operated in extraordinary power and authority as they prayed, spoke the Word, rebuked demons, and ministered to people.

However, most Christians struggle to believe that God has delegated the very same authority to them. It's just as available today as it was when Jesus or the first apostles walked the earth!

A common misconception is that we should pray and ask God or Jesus to heal the sick, cast out demons, or perform other miracles. So we pray nice religious prayers; and usually nothing happens when we pray like this.

In contrast, look what Jesus told His disciples:

As you go, preach, saying, "The kingdom of heaven is at hand." Heal the sick, cleanse the lepers, raise the dead, cast out demons. Freely you have received, freely give.   (Matthew 10:7–8)

Do you see how radical this word of instruction is? Jesus didn't tell them to pray for God to heal people or cast out demons; He told His disciples that they could do these things!

Likewise, part of the Great Commission involved God's people performing signs and wonders:

*These signs will follow **those who believe: In My name they** will cast out demons; **they** will speak with new tongues; **they** will take up serpents; and if **they** drink anything deadly, it will by no means hurt them; **they** will lay hands on the sick, and they will recover.*   (Mark 16:17–18)

Notice that Jesus didn't instruct us to pray that *He* would do these things. He said *we* could do these signs if we use the authority we have in *His* name! Perhaps you've never seen this amazing truth in Scripture before; but it will change your life when you do.

Crucified and Risen with Him

Often the problem with recognizing our authority is that we don't have a revelation of our identification and union with Christ. Paul explained it like this:

I have been crucified with Christ; it is no longer I who live, but Christ lives in me; and the life which I now live in the flesh I live by faith in the Son of God, who loved me and gave Himself for me. (Galatians 2:20)

Paul understood that we were crucified with Him, we were raised with Him, and now we are seated with Him in the heavenly places. Johnny Cash used to sing an old gospel song that asked,

Were you there when they crucified my Lord?
Were you there when they nailed him to the tree?
Were you there when they laid him in the tomb?
Were you there when God raised him from the tomb?

I happened to hear the song not long ago, and I felt like shouting at the top of my lungs, "*Yes*, I was there! And not only was I there, but I was crucified *with* Him and raised *with* Him. Now I have every spiritual blessing through my identification and union with Him at the Father's right hand."

Take a moment and let this sink in, my friend. If you are a believer, every victory Christ won has been credited to you. Because you were joined to Him, you were crucified, buried, and raised. (See Romans 6:3–5; Colossians 3:1–4.) Now you are seated with Him in heavenly places, far about any principality or power of the enemy. (See Ephesians 1:3, 19–23.) Although He is sitting at the right hand of the Father in heaven, you and I have His authority here on earth.

Living Above Our Circumstances

I once greeted a church member and asked him how he was doing.

"Oh, pretty good, under the circumstances," was his fainthearted reply.

"What are you doing under there?" I asked him with a chuckle.

You see, my friend, God has placed us in a position far above our problems and circumstances. The challenge is to *recognize* our position and *stay seated* where the

Lord has placed us. We must not allow ourselves to be pulled down into the realm of fear, anxiety, worry, depression, sickness, or disease.

The natural realm is Satan's arena. He plays his games in the realm of our five physical senses of seeing, hearing, tasting, touching, and smelling. He wins his battles by provoking us to walk "*by sight*" (2 Corinthians 5:7)—with our five senses—rather than by faith. He convinces us we are sick or dying or about to lose everything we own, and all the while we actually are seated with Christ in heavenly places.

We must begin to see things from Jesus' perspective rather than with our natural eyes. We must be able to judge natural things according to what God's Word says about our spiritual reality. When we begin to operate in our authority, far above any attacks in the natural realm, we start to conquer doubt and unbelief.

So, if we're waiting to *feel* our healing, we will keep waiting forever. But the breakthrough will come when we step out and say, "I am healed, whether I feel like it or not!" We can walk in that same authority when it comes to our finances, our families, or any other area of our lives.

Unclaimed Funds

Every so often, you'll see a news report on TV or in a newspaper about "unclaimed funds." Some of this money involves tax refunds people didn't realize they were entitled to. At other times, there are life insurance proceeds or probate bequests that have never been received by the intended beneficiary.

Friend, as a believer, you've been awarded an enormous inheritance. You are a joint heir with Jesus, God's dear Son. And in Him you have been blessed with "*every spiritual blessing in the heavenly places*" (Ephesians 1:3).

However, if you are like many Christians, your incredible inheritance is still hidden away in a spiritual bank account you've rarely, if ever, accessed. Perhaps you never even knew it was there.

Don't allow your "funds" to go unclaimed. God has put you in His "will," and He wants you to be blessed!

29

RESTORING THE DIVINE DESIGN

Picture yourself getting a knock on your door one day. It turns out to be a mail carrier with a certified letter you need to sign for. Perhaps you're fearful it's some kind of bad news or legal action; but then it turns out to be quite the opposite.

To your surprise, the letter says you've been discovered to be *royalty* and are entitled to a vast, unexpected inheritance. And the moment you sign, the inheritance is yours!

You're probably thinking my story is pretty far-fetched; but it's not. If you've been born again, you *are* royalty—a son or daughter of the King of the entire universe!

To understand what that means, we have to look back at the story of creation in the first three chapters of Genesis. Adam and Eve didn't have to create the garden of Eden; they were born into it. It was their rightful, God-ordained home.

The garden of Eden was a place of incredible abundance. There was no poverty, strife, sickness, or death. Before Adam and Eve sinned, they experienced a "no sweat" kind of life—the same kind of life God intends for you and me today.

Authority was a fundamental part of God's design in creating Adam and Eve:

*Then God said, "Let Us make man in Our image, according to Our likeness;
let them have **dominion** over the fish of the sea, over the birds of the air, and
over the cattle, over all the earth and over every creeping thing that creeps on the
earth." So God created man in His own image; in the image of God He created
him; male and female He created them. Then God blessed them, and God said
to them, "Be fruitful and multiply; fill ["replenish" KJV] the earth and **subdue** it;
have **dominion** over the fish of the sea, over the birds of the air, and over every
living thing that moves on the earth."* (Genesis 1:26–28)

God's original design for humankind was clear: We were made in His image,
created to have authority over all the earth, and expected to multiply and increase.

My friend, God's plan has never changed. He *still* wants us to be conformed to His
image (see Romans 8:29), and He *still* expects us to multiply and increase, expanding
His kingdom throughout the earth. But in many ways, both of these critical parts of
God's plan hinge on *restoring us to our proper place of authority*. Let me explain.

What Happened at the Fall?

God created Adam and Eve to take dominion and exercise authority over His
creation. This was an inherent part of their nature and their calling. However, in
order for them to *exercise* God's authority, they had to remain *under* His authority.

Satan, the serpent, recognized that if he could get Adam and Eve to disobey
God, they would forfeit their authority. Even worse, by listening to Satan instead of
God, they would, in effect, be placing themselves under Satan's authority.

As is almost always the case with his schemes, Satan's attack began with ques-
tioning and undermining God's Word: *"Has God indeed said...?"* (Genesis 3:1).
That's why it's so crucial to believe and obey God. When we doubt Him or disobey
Him, we're opening up our lives to the devil's snares.

Just as the Fall was caused by a violation of God's authority, restoration comes
when divine authority is regained in the life of a believer. And just as the Fall resulted
in the curse of sickness, death, emotional distress, relationship conflicts, and lack,
God wants to *reverse* these conditions when we step back under His authority. That's
why we're told, *"Submit to God. Resist the devil and he will flee from you"* (James 4:7).
The first step in regaining authority over Satan and our circumstances is *submitting
our lives fully to God.*

Never forget: Satan not only hates God, but he also hates people, since we were created in God's likeness. The devil is an outlaw spirit. He was cast out of heaven and will forever be an outcast.

It's interesting that Satan used the body of a serpent to tempt Eve and Adam. In Revelation 20:2, he is referred to as *"that serpent of old, who is the Devil and Satan."* Originally, the serpent was beautiful and walked upright. But after the incident in the garden, he was cursed and was forced to slither on his belly as a reptile.

When I see a snake, I think of the cunning serpent that did so much damage in the garden of Eden. However, we can't expect the devil to come to us today as a serpent, or a snake, or with a pitchfork in a red jumpsuit. Instead, the Bible tells us that *"Satan himself masquerades as an angel of light"* (2 Corinthians 11:14 NIV).

Yes, Lucifer is a master of disguise and deception, portraying himself as benevolent instead of malevolent, light instead of darkness. Fortunately, God can give us discernment, so we don't have to be fooled by Satan's trickery. (See 2 Corinthians 2:11.)

Replenishing the Earth

Part of our calling as humankind is to *"replenish the earth"* (Genesis 1:28 KJV). The Hebrew word for *"replenish"* is *male*, which means to fill, overflow, fulfill, satisfy, complete, or to consecrate.

God still wants us to be a part of replenishing the earth today, until it is *"filled with the knowledge of the glory of the LORD, as the waters cover the sea"* (Habakkuk 2:14). As believers, we can stand in our authority and bring fulfillment, satisfaction, completion, and consecration to this planet. We can play a role in bringing it back to display the glory He originally intended it to display.

How can we do that? you might wonder. Let me share a word picture that may help.

If you've ever stayed in an expensive hotel on the beaches of Florida or Hawaii, you've no doubt been impressed by the beautiful sand, water, palm trees, shrubs, and flowers. However, if you go down the road a little ways, you're likely to see a public beach that doesn't look anything like the lavish beach by the hotel. Why the difference? The beachfront near the hotel has been *replenished*. More sand was trucked in, new palm trees were planted, and landscaping companies have planted beautiful flowers and shrubbery.

The beach by the hotel didn't look as inviting until someone purchased the property and replenished it. This required an investment of time, resources, and creativity; but it surely was worth the effort. God has shown me that we need to have this kind of vision for exercising our dominion and authority on the earth. We are here to make a difference, in the lives of people and on the earth, as well.

God wants us to take *ownership* of the earth. Yes, we are stewards and caretakers, but we're also a lot more than that, as the psalmist declared: *"The heavens belong to the LORD, but he has given the earth to all humanity"* (Psalm 115:16 NLT). This is part of our amazing inheritance as *"heirs of God and joint heirs with Christ"* (Romans 8:17).

The way we see ourselves, whether as owners or just stewards, is important. Think of it this way: Do owners or tenants take better care of the houses they live in? Most renters aren't very motivated to improve and "replenish" the house or apartment where they live. If we're not the *owners*, we simply don't *care* as much.

All Things Made New

At the first creation, *"God saw everything that He had made, and indeed it was very good"* (Genesis 1:31). He hadn't created sin or suffering, poverty or disease. Think of it: *"everything"* he made *"was very good"*; but sin and rebellion changed all of this.

Fortunately, the story doesn't end there. In Christ, God brought about a *new* creation: *"If anyone is in Christ, he is a new creation; old things have passed away; behold, all things have become new"* (2 Corinthians 5:17).

What a wonderful turn of events for a believer! Just as everything was *"very good"* in the first creation, God reverses the curse on fallen humanity in the new creation and "makes all things new."

Friend, if you are "in Christ" today, this is your amazing royal inheritance! You don't have to accept your inheritance from Adam, because you've been adopted into the royal family line of the Son of God. You're a child of the King!

30

THE PAUPER WHO
HAD BEEN A PRINCE

Remember my story in the last chapter about unexpectedly receiving a notice that you were royalty? There's a story in the Bible that's a lot like that.

A man was living in squalor in a dry and desolate place called Lo Debar. Both of his feet crippled, life was extremely hard for him. With little hope of anything ever changing, he had become increasingly depressed and bitter.

But one day, some men came from Jerusalem with surprising news for this lame man, whose name was Mephibosheth: King David wanted to see him. The men picked up Mephibosheth and took him before the king.

At first, he wasn't certain what David's intentions were. After all, Mephibosheth was the grandson of King Saul and the son of Jonathan, who had been next in line for the throne before his death. This meant he was part of Saul's royal lineage, and he feared David would see him as a potential threat to his reign.

Though he had been living as a pauper, Mephibosheth actually was a prince. However, when he was just five years old, his father and grandfather both were killed while the nation was at war. As his nanny hurriedly took him to safety, she dropped the young boy, and he became lame. (See 2 Samuel 4:4.) After David secured the kingdom, Mephibosheth had fled in fear to Lo Debar, far away from the princely life he once knew.

It's easy to understand how Mephibosheth could have become bitter and hopeless. Fortunately, his story didn't end in Lo Debar—and *your* story doesn't need to end in defeat and despair, either!

Becoming a Prince Again

David didn't want to punish or kill Mephibosheth. Quite the contrary, he wanted to *bless* him—to *"show him kindness for Jonathan's sake"* (2 Samuel 9:1). Instead of being based on any particular merit or worthiness on the part of Mephiboseth, David's kindness and generosity were the result of his deep friendship with Jonathan, the young man's father. And so, despite Mephibosheth's fears and lousy self-image, David gave him some almost unbelievable news: *"[I] will restore to you all the land of Saul your grandfather"* (verse 7).

What a beautiful picture of our redemption in Christ! Like Mephibosheth, we come from a princely line, and we're destined to return to royalty. Yes, we were crippled by the fall, and, as a result, we're living in a barren place, far from the royal palace. But the King has intervened in our bleak circumstances. He is *restoring* us to the princely position that was lost!

Not only was Mephibosheth restored with his inheritance and his land, but King David treated him as a son: *"He shall eat at my table like one of the king's sons"* (2 Samuel 9:11). In the same way, God doesn't treat us a smelly old "sinner saved by grace"; He adopts us as His beloved sons and daughters. Instead of being beggars or paupers, we are called to eat *"continually at the king's table"* (verse 13). Isn't that exciting!

The Crumbs of the Kingdom

Mephibosheth didn't have to eat crumbs or leftovers from David's table; the whole feast was his! However, another story in Scripture illustrates that even the "crumbs" of God's kingdom are incredibly powerful.

In Matthew 15:21–31, a Canaanite woman cried out to Jesus, *"Have mercy on me, O Lord, Son of David! My daughter is severely demon-possessed"* (verse 22). The woman knew she had a serious need, and she knew that Jesus was the only one who could help her.

However, Jesus was intent on testing the Canaanite woman's faith. At first, *"He answered her not a word"* (Matthew 15:23), and His disciples urged Him to send the annoying woman away. Then He put another barrier in her way, saying that He was only sent *"to the lost sheep of the house of Israel"* (verse 24); and He added, *"It is not good to take the children's bread and throw it to the little dogs"* (verse 26).

But this woman didn't give up easily! She was persistent, and she finally discovered the key to getting what she needed from Him. She told Him, *"Yes, Lord, yet even the little dogs eat the crumbs which fall from their masters' table"* (verse 27).

What was the key to Jesus' heart? *Faith!* He immediately responded, ***"O woman, great is your faith! Let it be to you as you desire"*** (verse 28).

Whenever Jesus did miracles like this, there was a ripple effect throughout the countryside:

> *Then great multitudes came to Him, having with them the lame, blind, mute, maimed, and many others; and they laid them down at Jesus' feet, and He healed them. So the multitude marveled when they saw the mute speaking, the maimed made whole, the lame walking, and the blind seeing; and they glorified the God of Israel.*   (Matthew 15:30–31)

My friend, when you stand in your faith as a believer, you will begin to see miracles in your life. Not only that, but *others* will see those miracles too. People will marvel, and they will glorify God.

Restored to Authority

Some Christians have the terrible misconception that although God has saved them, they are still on some kind of "probation." As a result, they feel like they must walk on eggshells, fearing that they might incur God's wrath or even lose their salvation at any moment.

This is not the Father's desire for us at all. If the story of Mephibosheth wasn't enough, we can see God's perspective from the story of the Prodigal Son in Luke 15. After squandering his inheritance, the wayward younger brother had found himself

184 ⌒ *Believer's Authority*

in a pigpen. He had fallen so low that the pigs' food looked inviting to him, and he would have been happy just to be one of his father's hired servants.

Yet the Father *completely* forgave and embraced this young man. Not only that, but he also restored him to full sonship and authority. How do we know this? Because he immediately offered his wayward boy the best robe, a signet ring, new sandals, and a fatted calf—all emblems of royalty. (See Luke 15:22–23.) The repentant son wasn't reprimanded or put on probation. He was given full authority—and full affection—as a dear son of his father.

Friend, if you have given your life to Christ, you are not on probation! You are no longer under a curse or a cloud of God's disfavor. You are *"accepted in the Beloved"* (Ephesians 1:6), entitled to exercise your full authority as a child of God!

31

A BELIEVER'S ULTIMATE VICTORY

I f spiritual battles are raging in your life today, it may be easy to forget an important truth: If our lives belong to Christ, our ultimate victory is certain! Have you ever recorded a football game or some other sports event that you were too busy to watch when it aired live? When you finally sit down to watch it, the game is *already over*. You may be curious about how the game unfolded, but there's absolutely no doubt at that point about the outcome.

The final chapter of history has already been written. There's no question about who the ultimate Victor will be. In fact, the victory song in heaven has already been written: *"Alleluia! For the Lord God Omnipotent reigns!"* (Revelation 19:6).

Sure, there will be difficult battles along the way. At times, it may even seem as if the devil has gotten the upper hand. But he *hasn't*!

When the final trumpet sounds, our Lord Jesus will overwhelmingly triumph. Loud voices in heaven will declare the final outcome: *"The kingdoms of this world have become the kingdoms of our Lord and of His Christ, and He shall reign forever and ever!"* (Revelation 11:15).

The devil and his minions want you to believe that he is invincible. What a ridiculous lie! Quite the opposite of being invincible, Satan is *already defeated!*

Satan's defeat was foretold from the moment Adam and Eve fell. God told the devil in Genesis 3:15, *"I will put enmity between you and the woman, and between your seed and her Seed; He shall bruise your head, and you shall bruise His heel."* Long before Jesus defeated sin, death, and Satan on the cross, God could look down through the corridors of time and see the certainty of our redemption.

In 1 Corinthians 15, Paul contrasts the spiritual death that came through Adam with the resurrection life that is available to a believer in Jesus: *"Since by man came death, by Man also came the resurrection of the dead. For as in Adam all die, even so in Christ all shall be made alive"* (1 Corinthians 15:21–22).

Paul goes on to proclaim the glorious victory that will come when Christ returns at the end of the age: *"Then comes the end, when He delivers the kingdom to God the Father, when He puts an end to all rule and all authority and power. For He must reign till He has put all enemies under His feet"* (verses 24–25).

You see, *"the end"* of the story has already been written—and Jesus wins! His victory will be so complete that He will destroy all competing rule, authority, or power. And He won't stop until *all* His enemies have been made a footstool for His feet!

It's sad today that some teachers of Bible prophecy seem to spend most of their time talking about the Antichrist and other end-time enemies, when that is not the focus of biblical prophecy at all. We're told in Revelation 19:10, *"The testimony of Jesus is the spirit of prophecy,"* and that is a *victorious* testimony, my friend.

This will not only be a victory for Jesus. As believers, it will be our victory, too. Jesus told us in Matthew 16:18 that the gates of hell would never, ever, ever prevail against His church! The word "gates" refers to authority. Jesus' message was that the "authority of hell" would never overpower the believing church.

Conquering Death, the Last Enemy

Paul describes the final enemy that will be destroyed at Jesus' return:

The last enemy that will be destroyed is death….For this corruptible must put on incorruption, and this mortal must put on immortality. So when this corruptible has put on incorruption, and this mortal has put on immortality, then shall be brought to pass the saying that is written: "Death is swallowed up in victory. O

Death, where is your sting? O Hades, where is your victory?"

(1 Corinthians 15:26, 53–55)

This final triumph over death is confirmed in John's beautiful revelation of the life that awaits us in eternity:

*I heard a loud voice from heaven saying, "Behold, the tabernacle of God is with men, and He will dwell with them, and they shall be His people. God Himself will be with them and be their God. And God will wipe away every tear from their eyes; there shall be **no more death**, nor sorrow, nor crying. There shall be no more pain, for the former things have passed away" Then He who sat on the throne said, "**Behold, I make all things new.**"* (Revelation 21:3–5)

What John is describing is the complete and total restoration of everything Adam and Eve lost when they sinned: Unhindered fellowship with God, and no more tears, death, sorrow, crying, or pain. What a day that will be!

However, some Christians are so focused on their heavenly home that they've missed out on God's amazing promises for a more "heavenly" life *today*. The message Jesus and the apostles preached was, *"Repent, for the kingdom of heaven is at hand"* (Matthew 4:17). This wasn't referring to an opportunity for people to escape this world and "go to heaven" soon. Quite the contrary; it meant that God wanted to touch people's earthly lives with the awesome blessings of His heavenly kingdom.

You see, when we submit ourselves to *heaven's authority* today, we can experience some of *heaven's benefits*. What does that mean? In heaven, there is no sickness, poverty, or strife. All things are made new by God's glorious presence.

And the good news is that His kingdom and His presence are already *"at hand"* today—right there with you. This means that if you are struggling in your family, health, or finances, heaven's resources are available for you to use. One touch from heaven can change everything!

God of the NOW

Many Christians struggle to see God in the *present*. Of course, they are certain He did great miracles in Bible days. And they likewise are convinced that mighty miracles will occur when Jesus returns. But *today* is a different matter. It's hard for them to believe that God intervenes in the "here and now" circumstances of their lives.

This is a tragic mistake.The very definition of faith includes the word *now*: "**Now** *faith is the substance of things hoped for, the evidence of things not seen*" (Hebrews 11:1). Did you catch that? Faith is a "*now*" kind of thing. It's wonderful to believe in God's past or future miracles, but He also wants us to believe Him to intervene in our lives in supernatural ways *today*.

Faith enables us to *see* the *unseen*. (See 2 Corinthians 4:18.) But notice that I didn't say faith will enable us to see "unreal" things that don't actually exist. Faith merely gives us the ability to see with the eyes of our heart into the spiritual realm and lay hold of what the Bible says already belongs to us. When we believe God's promises and release them through our words, we will eventually see them manifested in our lives.

But Paul wrote, "*We walk by faith, not by sight*" (2 Corinthians 5:7). I once heard a minister give an example of this, explaining that there's a difference in believing in your *heart*, believing in your *head*, and believing in only what you *see*. What a contrast! If we base our lives on "*sight*" (or our other limited sensory perceptions), there's no way we can walk in faith.

Resurrection Life

In the story of Lazarus' resurrection in John 11, we can see the importance of believing God in the "present tense." First, notice that Jesus made sure He arrived at His friend's tomb after Lazarus was already dead and buried. This was infuriating to Martha and Mary, Lazarus' sisters, and each of them told Jesus, "*Lord, if You had been here, my brother would not have died*" (John 11:21, 32). These two sisters claimed to have had perfect faith that Jesus could have healed their brother—if only He had arrived in time. So they were believers in Jesus' power to perform *healing*, but they weren't quite so sure about *resurrection*.

Notice that their faith initially extended to the past and the future, just not the present. They chided Jesus for not showing up sooner, for surely He would have been able to do something to heal their brother in the past. And then, when Jesus told Martha, "Your brother will rise again" (John 11:23), Martha immediately jumped to the future: "*I know that he will rise again in the resurrection at the last day*" (verse 24).

But look how Jesus turned this around by using the *present* tense: "*I **am** the resurrection and the life. He who believes in Me, though he may die, he shall live*" (John 11:25). Friend, Jesus is your great "I *am*" today! Whatever miracle you need from Him, you can ask Him in faith today! Remember this great truth: "*Jesus Christ is the same yesterday, today, and forever*" (Hebrews 13:8).

If You Believe

Martha and Mary initially blamed Jesus for their brother's death. The Lord had been a close friend of Lazarus and the family. He used to stay at their home when He was nearby. He had shared the Word with them, and they believed in Him—yet he had let their brother die.

This must have been a heart-wrenching scene. Not only were Martha and Mary weeping, but a crowd of others had gathered around to weep and lament their friend's death. Confronted with all these distraught, bewildered, and angry people, Jesus "*groaned in the spirit and was troubled*" (John 11:33).

People have different explanations for why Jesus groaned and was troubled, but I think the key may found in verse 40: "*Jesus said to [Martha], 'Did I not say to you that if you would **believe** you would **see** the glory of God?'*" This is such a beautiful verse, packed with insights about a believer's authority. Let's take a closer look at the main operative words used in this passage:

- **You.** Martha and Mary were mad that Jesus didn't do something to keep their brother from dying. However, Jesus turned the focus back to *their* faith. Over the years, I've seen so many Christians who are like Martha and Mary, upset that God didn't show up and fix their situation. But what they fail to grasp is that Jesus lives in them. Their miracle was well within reach, but they had to exercise their own faith and stand in their authority as believers.

- **Believe.** While Martha and Mary wanted to talk about the past or the future, Jesus kept bringing them back to faith in the *present tense*. No matter what the situation (and how stinky their brother's corpse may have become after four days), God can still be glorified by a great miracle if we believe Him *now*.

- **See.** You've no doubt heard people use the old maxim, "Seeing is believing." But actually, the opposite is true: Believing *precedes* seeing. If you are waiting to see something before you start believing, you will be waiting a *long* time! But it's also important to understanding that believing doesn't *make* something true. It is already true, but believing enables us to have our spiritual eyes enlightened to that truth.

+ **Glory.** God's glory is the visible revelation of His *invisible* attributes and majesty. He wants to show off His glory through the lives of His people: *"Arise, shine; for your light has come! And the glory of the LORD is risen upon you"* (Isaiah 60:1). We should be so filled with God's Spirit that *everything* we do is a demonstration of His glory. (See 1 Corinthians 10:31.)

+ **If.** Of course, *"if"* was the very first word in Jesus' promise here. Throughout the Bible, God gives us fantastic promises. But in nearly every case, the promise comes with a *condition*—some kind of *"if."* God's blessings are virtually unlimited for the Christian, but only *"if"* he or she believes Him and appropriates those blessings.

I'm always amazed when I meet people who have trusted God with their eternal salvation but who struggle to trust Him with the lesser issues of life. If they would believe, they could see God's glory manifested in their health, their finances, their family, their ministry, and every other part of their lives. But, like Martha and Mary, they struggle to believe God for His miracles in the "here and now" circumstances they encounter.

I remember talking with a friend who refused to fly on airplanes. Although he was a Christian, with assurance of a heavenly home if he died, he simply couldn't trust God to keep him safe on a plane. He had claimed the Bible's promises about being born again, but he somehow couldn't claim the promises about being *"anxious for nothing"* (Philippians 4:6).

It doesn't have to be this way, my friend. *If* you believe God to intervene in *any* area of your life, you can see His glory and His provision revealed in that area.

The God Who Raises the Dead

Paul wrote to the Corinthians, *"We should not trust in ourselves but in God who raises the dead"* (2 Corinthians 1:9). There is such a wonderful principle here. No matter what kind of battle you may be facing today in your health, finances, or relationships, nothing is too hard for the Lord. He not only can heal the sick, but He also can raise the *dead*—and that includes "dead" ministries, marriages, and financial outlooks.

Years ago, I was called to the hospital by a pastor whose three-year-old son had just drowned. This man called together eight other ministers, and we all prayed in a private room for the boy to be raised from the dead.

After several hours, in great anguish, the boy's father called a halt to our prayers. Breaking down in tears, he thanked us all for coming, and we comforted him as much as we could before leaving. But as we were walking out, several of the pastors behind me said, "I don't really know why we came. I never did think the boy could be raised."

These men should not have come to pray that day. Although they were believers, they didn't believe God could and would raise this little boy from the dead. Do you see why Jesus was selective about who was allowed to go with Him when He raised Jairus' daughter from the dead in Luke 8:49–56? He had been told not to bother coming to the girl's bedside, for she was already dead. But He replied, *"Do not be afraid; only believe, and she will be made well"* (Luke 8:50).

But despite Jesus' warning here about fear and unbelief, He realized that some people would still pollute the atmosphere with doubt. As a result, *"He permitted no one to go in except Peter, James, and John, and the father and mother of the girl"* (verse 51). Jesus didn't raise the girl from the dead until He had first *"put them* [those who did not believe] *all outside"* (verse 54).

You see, both faith and unbelief are powerful forces. Never forget Jesus' words at Lazarus' tomb: *"If you would **believe** you would see the glory of God"* (John 11:40).

Keep believing God, my friend. Keep standing in your authority as a believer. All things are possible when you believe!

ABOUT THE AUTHOR

In 1979, God spoke to Happy Caldwell to build a spiritual production center in Little Rock, Arkansas, in order to take the good news of Jesus Christ to the city, state, nation, and world. Happy and his wife, Jeanne, founded Agape Church, a strong, spirit-filled body of believers. Through his deep sensitivity to the Spirit of God and his anointed teaching, the lost are being saved, the sick are being healed, and thousands are being blessed.

In 1988, Happy and Jeanne answered a direct call from the Lord to take His message beyond Central Arkansas. They founded VTN—the Victory Television Network. This network of three full-power TV stations is carried on more than two hundred cable systems and is bringing the gospel into more than 1.2 million households. Through his own daily program, *Arkansas Alive*, Happy presents the Word in profound simplicity, making the character of God a revelation to those who hear.

Also desiring to see spiritual excellence in education, the ministry of Agape has grown to include Agape Academy and Agape College, which offers both diploma and degree programs.

Happy's ministry is known for instilling Christian principles in strategic leadership. He was honored for this in 2005 with an invitation to participate in the US Army War College Strategic Leader Staff Ride at Gettysburg, Pennsylvania.

He is a recipient of the Peter J. Daniels Caleb Encourager Award, which has been bestowed upon such notable people as Norman Vincent Peale, Nelson Mandela, and Dr. Oral Roberts. He has also been recognized by the Arkansas Martin Luther King Jr. Commission with The Salute to Greatness Community Service Award.

Happy Caldwell continues to travel worldwide delivering the life-changing message of Jesus Christ. He has recorded several albums with Jeanne and has written several books, including *Saving Our Cities*, *An Expected End*, and *How to Thrive in Perilous Times*.